THE GURU ON THE MOUNTAIN

THE GURU ON THE MOUNTAIN

Chiggers, Lizards & Desert Heat:
My Vision Quest to
Discover the Source of Spirit

Darrell G. Yardley

New Insights Press

Editorial Direction and Editing: Rick Benzel
Copy editing: Julie Simpson, OnWords and UpWords!
Back cover photo: Noelle Yardley
Cover and Book Design: Josep Book Designs

Published by New Insights Press, Los Angeles, CA

First edition printed in the United States of America

ISBN: 978-1-7338411-9-1 (print)

Library of Congress Control Number: 2020911374

DEDICATION

To spiritual seekers everywhere and my family.

TABLE OF CONTENTS

PROLOGUE

IF YOU ARE INTERESTED IN YOUR OWN SPIRITUALITY AND SPIRITUAL growth, in gaining a deeper understanding of why spirituality is important to humans, and in learning what might be the underlying science of spirituality, read on.

This is primarily my story about a Native American (Plains Indian) four-day desert vision quest I undertook years ago. It also combines snapshots, incidents, and insights from several other intensive spiritual retreats I have taken over the decades, mainly Zen Buddhist *sesshins*. Those, for me, were brutal and powerful, as was the vision quest. These types of experiences push you out of your comfort zone and stimulate neurogenesis (brain growth). It is there that real and rapid spiritual growth can occur.

I define spirituality as a combination of inner peace and personal growth. Here I define inner peace in a Buddhist sense, as the end of suffering; Buddha taught about what causes our suffering and how to end it. As for personal growth, a vast and probably endless process, here I am focusing on understanding and using archetypes as an aspect of the Jungian process of individuation. Our archetypes are real but operate primarily at the subconscious level. They are creatures of our species' genes and the evolutionary process. They were the spirit guides or allies of indigenous shamans and peoples. Through my story, I invite you to meet and make use of your own archetypes, as they are metaphors and symbols with emotional content and meaning that can help you solve problems and deal more effectively with your life challenges.

With my background as a professor of science (zoology, specializing in evolutionary genetics) and later in my life as a mental health therapist (Licensed Professional Counselor), I have a unique perspective on how the sciences in general, and particularly evolutionary biology, can give us deeper insights into the spiritual growth process. These insights are more like hypotheses, but hypotheses that you can test for yourself in your own spiritual journey. Some of the science I will discuss is pretty heavy. There is no way around this if you are to understand what I am saying and why. At the same time, I did not want the science to get too much in the way of the story itself. Finding this balance was more than challenging, sort of like the vision quest itself.

Likewise, there is a little math. Now before you run away screaming, let me assure you I have tried to keep the math to a minimum. But the truth is, the great power of science lies in its math and testable hypotheses. Charles Darwin, for example, would not have been able to formulate his theory of evolution by natural selection if it had not been for a critical book by Thomas Malthus, entitled *An Essay on Principles of Populations*. Like Darwin, Malthus was a cleric and scholar, and his book asserted that, mathematically, the population of any species should quickly overwhelm the world with its growth. Darwin posited that the reason this did not occur was due to natural selection: that is, a lot of those offspring did not survive. That took math to figure out.

Although I have framed my vision quest around the Native American medicine wheel's four directions, the science I introduce in my story was a later addition, wrapped around the actual desert experience itself. It was all I could do to get through those four days of intense heat, isolation, lack of food, very limited water, and the mosquitoes. I knew a lot of the science, but that was definitely not what I was out there thinking about. The science was woven into this story years later as I reflected back on my experience. The last two key pieces that pulled it together for me were the underlying neurobiology of archetypes (and gods) and dissipation-driven adaptation from physics. I had not learned about these until years after my quest, when relevant writings were published.

Enjoy your read and the journey....

PART ONE

The Vision Quest

TURTLE ROCK: RUNNIN' ON INDIAN TIME

ARRIVAL IN SAN ANTONIO, AUGUST 2004

MEETING ME AT THE SAN ANTONIO AIRPORT ON SATURDAY MORNING were Grandfather Chasing Thunder and Ann, one of my fellow questees. I learned that Grandfather Chasing Thunder would be assisting Strong Eagle in our vision quests. None of us had previously met, but since I was the only passenger sporting a large backpack and camping gear coming off the plane, it was easy for them to pick me out. I was lucky my sleeping bag made it because the security people went through it but couldn't figure out how to (or did not want to take the time to) reattach it to my backpack. It appeared on the baggage rack trailing my backpack like a dog on a long leash.

Strong Eagle was a Native American medicine man. Half Ute, he had master's degrees in anthropology and nursing, was a teacher of the Native American tradition, and facilitated vision quests, especially in the Big Bend area of Texas. He also was a desert survival enthusiast—well, actually more of a fanatic. Compared to me, he was tall. He was also thirty years younger. With dark hair and skin, and a different physiology apparently, he seemed well suited for the desert environment. I would find that he was almost immune to the desert's heat, exceedingly

1

able to handle it, while I would be wilting, desperate to find some shade and coolness.

We arrived at Strong Eagle's home several hours later, where, after being introduced to his family and other members of our expedition, his wife, Denise, took me aside and asked for my wristwatch. As I handed it to her, no doubt looking puzzled, she said, "You're running on Indian time now. I will give this back when you return."

Academically, I knew what Indian time was but for the next seven days I was going to find out firsthand—experientially. After several trips into Mexico, I understood Mexican time: *mañana*, literally translated as "tomorrow," meant in real-life time, "later," which in turn often meant "never." Indian time was different. Indian time meant "it gets done when it gets done" or "in its own time." Actually, living on Indian time was quite a culture shock for me.

The handing over of my watch was just one step in the severance process one needs to go through in preparation for a vision quest. That evening, we would be participating in an *inipi* (sweat lodge) ceremony, marking the official start of our vision quests. The purpose of the ceremony was to cleanse us for the start of our quest. It was a rite of purification. You have to let go of your old life in order to be reborn into a new life. Having left my family and life back in South Carolina, I had severed myself from my former life, if only temporarily. There was a certain anxiety that accompanied this separation. I was apprehensive about the next seven days (including my travel days) that I would be away from home and what laid in wait for me out in the desert. And I should have been. If I had known what was coming, I would have clambered back onto that plane!

A vision quest is a sacred Native American ceremony. Traditionally, it involves four days of isolation in nature without food, water, or sleep, with only a blanket as a shield from the weather. My first quest in 1999, in the deserts of New Mexico, had been for only one day, a little over 24 hours. This was the more traditional four-day one. However, because the Texan desert was so extreme, Strong Eagle had taken mercy on us. We "questees" would each be allowed to take three gallons of water and a tarp, as well as a sleeping pad and blanket, out on our quests.

The purpose of a vision quest was just that—to get a vision of your life: where you were in it, where you wanted to go with it, and what you needed to let go of, let die. Originally used as a rite of passage for young braves into adulthood, the vision quest facilitated a youth's understanding about who he was and his role in the tribe. In Native American tradition, vision quests could also be used during times of passage or transitions in one's life to gain clarity and perspective.

Strong Eagle had emailed me some five months earlier, inviting me to participate in this vision quest, knowing that I had wanted to do one in the Big Bend, Texas area for several years. I immediately accepted. There were four questees: Ann, Kelon, Travis, and myself. Youngsters, all of them. I was the old man of the group.

Ernie, who was helping Strong Eagle with the quest, was actually a couple of years older than I. He was tall, slim, had a thin, drooping mustache and a twinkle in his eye. Soft-spoken and thoughtful, his persona spoke of the desert stillness itself. His Indian name, Grandfather Chasing Thunder, was derived from his own vision quest with Strong Eagle several years prior when a major lightning and thunderstorm occurred. Lightening was flashing all around, striking the ground in the desert mountains about him, and the crazy fool went out chasing it! It was a wonder he did not get fried, tostada style.

Our quest was to be held the first week of August. A whole week in the desert mountains of far southwest Texas. I shot back an email to Strong Eagle, "Couldn't you find a hotter date?" (July and August are the hottest times in Big Bend. Temperatures can get up to 115°F!) Strong Eagle answered back, "Well, it might be a little warm." Ha!, a gross understatement.

I hate heat. Let's be perfectly clear about that. I have Celtic DNA and fair skin that doesn't take to a lot of sunshine. I like cool or cold weather. But despite my genes, I am drawn to the desert, especially the high desert mountains of Texas, New Mexico, and Arizona. What a contradiction: I love the desert but hate its high heat.

My desert "attraction" is, in large part I am sure, due to my growing up in the high desert of West Texas, in Odessa, some 250 miles from Big Bend. It was hot in the desert, but dry. When I revisited the desert high plains those days leading up to the quest, my soul sang. I could breathe. The desert was my home. In the desert I felt like a caged bird released into the air.

As a boy growing up in the desert, I came to appreciate its subtle beauty, its rugged wildlife, and its harsh conditions. When our children were little and we occasionally came out to the desert, my family could not understand the desert's attraction for me. They all grew up in the southeast, where you cannot see the sunset for the trees.

Don't get me wrong. I love trees. I loved our small farm in South Carolina. But, God, sometimes I ached for the wide-open spaces of my desert home. So now, for this vision quest, I felt like I had come home— and it was about to beat the living crap out of me.

Odessa is on the high desert plain, but not in the mountains themselves. For mountains, you have to travel farther southwest to where the Davis Mountains jut out from the tail end of the Rockies, or further south to the Chisos Mountains. There are also the Guadalupe Mountains in between.

As when on the ocean, in the desert you can see the horizon. The setting and rising sun are visible for a hundred miles. The sky is open, blue, and dotted with white fluffy clouds in the day; the stars and moon, big and bright at night. I feel closer to God, more connected to the cosmos and creation. It is expansive, not confining. The desert is a place of cleansing, of renewal, of getting back to basics, the primal. That was what I needed in my life.

Jesus and the Desert Fathers of Egypt all went into the desert. Many other great teachers spent time in their own deserts; Mohammed and

Buddha come to mind. These examples inspired me. Not that I had any aspirations to become a great teacher, though. Hell, I was just trying to get my shit together!

We spent several hours that first afternoon gathering wood and preparing for the *inipi* ceremony. Strong Eagle's house, located in the hill country near Hunt, Texas, was surrounded by an abundance of cedar and juniper trees. I waded through the knee-high prairie grass gathering firewood for the fire that would heat the stones for our ceremony. Strong Eagle already had a pile of stones ready. They would be placed in the fire later in the afternoon.

The sweat lodge itself was a traditional low dome-shaped structure about five feet tall at its highest center point. Constructed from a frame of tree trunks and branches, it was covered with several layers of blankets, except for a small opening on one side that functioned as the door. All along its edges where the blankets meet the ground were heaps of dirt to help seal the heat inside. Our sweat lodge was about ten feet in diameter. In the center was a pit where the glowing hot stones would be placed. The stones were about the size of a person's head or a little smaller.

In the gathering dusk, we entered one by one through the low opening, bowing down and touching the ground as we said *mitakuye oyasin*, which is Lakota Sioux for "all my relations." In the small structure, we sat shoulder to shoulder, touching each other. It was dark inside.

Grandfather Chasing Thunder dug the large stones out of the burning embers with a pitchfork. They glowed and smoked as he carefully handed them on the pitchfork one by one to Strong Eagle, who placed each one in the pit and then handed the pitchfork back to

Grandfather to get the next one. With each stone, the heat inside the lodge started to climb. He placed four stones into the pit. Grandfather came in and sat down near the door, then closed it. We were plunged into blackness except for the orange-red glow emanating from the heated stones.

The heat from the rocks radiated intensely, burning the skin on my legs, which were closest to the pit. I rocked backwards, recoiling and trying to pull my bare legs away from the hot stones. I knew what was coming! The temperature escalated exponentially in the closed structure. Strong Eagle sprinkled aromatic herbs of sage and sweet grass on the hot, glowing stones. They burned instantly as they hit, their fragrant smoke filling the air around us. He then poured several large ladles of water on the rocks. Steam sizzled, hot water spat. I groaned and tried to inhale. The hot, steam-saturated air burned the lining of my nose. It scorched my throat. Breathing it in, it made my lungs feel as if they were boiling. I threw my t-shirt over my head to act as a filter, cooling the air a little to a more breathable temperature. It helped, but only slightly. But my t-shirt was too hot to keep against my face. There was nowhere to go; no place to hide. The heat was relentless, unyielding, unforgiving—an omen of things to come for my vision quest.

Strong Eagle beat a rhythm on his large ceremonial drum and asked a blessing from the East, the direction of rebirth and vision. We each added our individual prayers for that direction. After what seemed like forever, the first round ended, the door was thrown open. The cool air rushed in and felt sweet, forgiving, wonderful!

But, alas, it was only a brief respite as Grandfather got up, went out, and started to retrieve the second round of hot stones from the fire. I shook my head; three more rounds to go. I winced. I would have cried, but it would do no good.

By the end of the second round, I was hugging the earthen floor, trying to find cooler air to breath. By the third round, my nose was buried in the dirt near the edge of the lodge. By the fourth round, I was nearly delirious. Forty-five minutes from the start of the ceremony, we emerged from the sweat lodge. Stepping out and drying off with a towel, the air was wonderfully clean and cool as I pulled it deep into my lungs. Ever so thankful to be breathing it, I felt clean as the cool night air evaporated the remaining sweat from my skin. My mind was clear, quiet, calm. The night sky was filled with beautiful stars. It was a peaceful feeling. I was ravenous. *This* was the feeling of purification.

Ceremonies and rites are important in any spiritual practice. They help connect us to the sacred and remind us that we are part of something bigger than ourselves. In Christianity, the Eucharist and baptism are ceremonies that point us in the spiritual direction. The same for Native American ceremonies, which act as doorways to the spiritual. Buddhism too has many such ceremonies with rites and rituals embedded: Buddha Day, Sangha (community) Day, Dhamma (teaching) Day, are examples. It was perhaps due to my own failings that I had experienced difficulties connecting to the spiritual in Christian ceremonies. I am not sure why.

Ceremonies remind us of the deeper meanings of life. They make us aware of the interconnectedness of life. In Christianity, this interconnectedness is with God and community. In Native American spirituality, this interconnectedness is with the Creator (a.k.a. God), each other (community), but also all of creation or nature (all our relations). In some forms of Christianity, e.g., Celtic, creation-centered, and certain others, our interconnection to all three is equally honored. In Buddhism, the interconnected is with Dharma (ultimate truth), Sangha (community), and Buddha and his teaching.

Strong Eagle was a great believer in ceremonies. The vision quest and the *inipi* ceremony are two of the seven Native American sacred rites or ceremonies. The four of us doing our quests each had to come up with a ceremony to perform when we got to our quest site to begin our quests. We were to have this ceremony prepared before our arrival there. I did.

If I had the wrong genes for the desert, I certainly had the wrong genes for the Native American *inipi* ceremony. It was the heat, combined with the humidity, that killed me in the sweat lodge. Not so with Strong Eagle. He seemed unfazed and immune to the searing heat. He sat in the hottest place in the lodge and conducted the ceremony. The hottest place was directly across from the opening, with the fire between him and the opening. Even sitting in the coolest place, which was near the door, I struggled to hang in there.

Following the sweat lodge, we had a replenishing dinner that Denise had prepared. After the meal and a little chitchat with my fellow questees, I found a quiet corner, unrolled my sleeping bag and pad, and was asleep in minutes. It had been a long day for me between my air and land travel. Besides, I was an early riser, often waking up on my own around 5:00 a.m. No alarm clock needed. Late into the night, I could hear Strong Eagle and the others talking as I weaved in and out of dream sleep.

The next morning (Sunday), I jumped awake scratching furiously at my legs. Pulling the covers back, I saw my legs, where they were covered by socks yesterday, were covered with angry, red, itching welts. Chiggers, the larval form of mites, I knew. They inject an enzyme into the skin and feed on the dead tissue it causes. Saying something about my prolific bites to Strong Eagle as I got up, he said, "Oh, yeah, there are a lot of chiggers out in the tall grass. Sorry, meant to tell you about that." I went to my backpack and retrieved an old tube of hydrocortisone cream and applied it. After a while, it eased my itching a little, but not much. Chiggers and mosquitoes loved me for some reason.

As we gathered around the breakfast table, Strong Eagle said he wanted to get started earlier on the drive to Big Bend than he did last year. Earlier than what time, I wondered? I discretely asked Denise. She said last year they started out around 10:00 p.m. "Ugh," I thought, "that's my bedtime. What's wrong with these people?" I said nothing of course. We spent all day packing two trucks. Tents, water, firewood (where we were going there would be little-to-no firewood), food, cots for sleeping (for Strong Eagle and Grandfather Chasing Thunder), tools, the list went on and on. While all this was happening, Denise called each of the questees aside to do a reading.

When it was my turn for a reading, I sat down on a blanket in front of Denise. She smudged both of us and the air around with sage. After a few moments of quietness and focus, she picked up a plastic bag she had prepared for me and emptied its contents onto the blanket. In the bag were bones of a turtle's shell and part of a rib, and a small cloth-stuffed turtle. (Little did I know she was presenting me with an omen about the place where I would do my quest, a place I would name Turtle Rock when I found it the next day.) She explained about turtle medicine.

Turtle is an ancient symbol for Mother Earth. From Mother Earth we are born and to her we shall return. From "dust to dust," as the Bible says. As Denise spoke, my thoughts flashed back to a vision I had several years before, of my being directly birthed from Mother Earth, from water and the desert soil. This ancient goddess energy asks us to give back to Mother Earth as she had given to us. Turtle asks us to honor our creativity, be grounded to the Earth, and see our lives with motherly compassion.

Denise asked me to select a medicine card. These were cards with pictures of various animals on them. Each animal represents a different type of "medicine" that is characteristic of that particular animal. In Native American spirituality, medicine is anything that improves one's connection to and understanding of the great mystery; of life and creation and the Creator.[1] It also includes healing or anything that brings personal power, strength, or understanding.

Each animal has its own unique medicine. By paying attention to its behavior and ecology, we could learn something about the medicine and teachings it gives to us. When we call on that animal's medicine, we learn lessons on how to live and to be from its perspective.

Many indigenous cultures believe we each have a power animal, which reflects something about our strengths and weaknesses. We also have additional animal guides, each of whose medicines serves us. Knowing our power animal tells us something about who we really are. Knowing our other animal guides encourages us to look at the world, our lives, and our situation from their medicine perspective.

We can see the legacy of the importance of these traditional animal guides in the many totems in our history and even in our modern world; e.g., in our national symbols, our sports teams' mascots, and in our colloquial speech. The national symbols of the United States and Russia, the eagle and bear, respectively, are examples. The Chicago Bears, the Detroit Lions, and from my own life, the Permian High School Panthers (see the book, TV show, and movie *Friday Night Lights*), the University of Texas Longhorns, the University of Georgia Bulldogs, and the Clemson University Tigers. Jesus had two totems: he was known as the Lamb of God and as the Lion of Judea. The lion was the totem of his tribe. Each of the twelve tribes of Israel had their own totems.

I reached into Denise's spread of cards and drew a black bear— the Lakota symbol of the west, one of the four cardinal directions in Native American spirituality. Bear medicine is about the power of introspection. I smiled. "Yes, I'll be doing a lot of introspection in the next several days." (What I didn't yet appreciate was just how intense that introspection would be. But then, this was what I came for.) She cautioned me that, although I might think after my quest that I had not received the answers I sought, those answers would surely be there. Out on the desert, I, of course, forgot all about her admonition, but her words would prove to have great truth.

THE JOURNEY BEGINS

We finally set out from Strong Eagle's house around 8:30 p.m. that evening, an hour-and-a-half earlier than Strong Eagle had left with his previous vision quest group. We stopped in Del Rio for breakfast around 1:30 a.m. Monday morning. In true southern tradition, I had country fried steak, mashed potatoes and gravy, eggs, and biscuits. I knew it would be the last real food I would be eating for several days.

We stopped at Walmart and loaded up on supplies. I bought the strongest anti-itching cream they had, remembering how in Mexico I was able to walk into a pharmacy and get 20% cream. Man, that stuff was wonderful. I was wishing I had it now, my itching legs were driving me so crazy.

What I realized already on this trip was that I was a morning person in a group of night owls. My circadian rhythm (wake-sleep cycle) was way out of sync with my fellow questees.

Another thing I realized was that the others were cigarette smokers. The exceptions were Ann and I, and she was thinking about starting. She was the youngest of the group, in her freshman year in college. Even though the windows were cracked as we drove to let in air and let out the dangerous second-hand smoke, I struggled with it all night. I couldn't get away from it in the enclosed truck. It brought up bad childhood memories of long drives with my parents, both of them smoking cigarette after cigarette in an enclosed car, and the resulting lung damage I received from it as a child. I was not happy but said nothing and sat by a cracked window the entire trip.

Arriving in the Big Bend area around 6:00 a.m., we crashed for a few hours of sleep, throwing our bedrolls down on a dirt road turnoff just outside of Terlingua. As dawn arrived, we were attacked by a hoard of hungry mosquitoes; another bad omen of things to come.

A couple of hours and several mosquito bites later, I stood looking southward toward Mexico in the early morning light. Turning in a circle, I was surrounded by desert and mountains on all sides. I looked down and beside my boot was a large black, gray, and brown tarantula crawling up the slope toward me. "Good morning, Mr. Tarantula," I said to him. We did not have tarantulas where I lived in South Carolina. At least I had never seen one there.

But a memory came back to me. I was a teen visiting my grandparents in Stephenville, Texas. I was driving my grandfather out to my uncle's farm in Granddad's little Ford Falcon, a barren model of a car by today's standards. They had had a local outbreak of tarantulas. Tarantulas were everywhere on the road. I gave up trying to miss them and just got used to the thud-squish sound as my tires flattened them against the pavement. I have never seen such an outbreak again. Looking back, it was pretty amazing.

Now, watching the tarantula as he made his way up the slope toward me, I was struck by how his long hairy legs encircled the hairy core of his body, his center, known as the cephalothorax. This was the heart and soul of the little guy. It contained his brain, stomach, mouth, and so forth. His abdomen, behind his cephalothorax, contained his gut, reproductive organs, and silk-spinning apparatus.

I turned my attention back to the road winding off in a distorted spiral before me. In the dark it had looked like a dirt road, but in the morning light it turned out to be a caliche road. It was more of a wagon trail than road at best. "Caliche," I thought. "The stuff of my childhood." I reached down and fingered the familiar chalky gravel. Caliche, for those who did not grow up in West Texas or New Mexico, is a deposit of calcium carbonate that is often seen as a white surface coating in dry regions. Instead of coating roads with gravel as they do in the east and other regions of the U.S., caliche is used. It also yields an instant road by just grading areas where it occurs naturally.

The caliche was a metaphor for me, I thought: Mother Earth was offering us a path if we but looked under the surface of things. A road provided for the asking. Giving us what we needed to find our way. I hoped I could see her "road" for my own life over the next few days.

Base Camp and Our Quest Sites

Back in the trucks, we followed the caliche road southward for twenty or so miles, heading into the rugged back country for over an hour. Because of washouts from the recent rains, we had to get out and rebuild the road in several places, using the abundant limestone rocks and flagstones that lay nearby. Finally, we arrived at the location of our base camp, which looked to me just like the desert we had been driving through for the past hour. Strong Eagle explained to us how to clear places for our tents and the main camp tent. We began unloading the two trucks and got to work.

The base camp was really out in the middle of nowhere, and a very dry, hot nowhere at that. It was located somewhere just outside of the Big Bend National Park, abutting its western side. To my east, I could see the Christmas Mountains. From studying a map before I came, I knew we were southwest of the Rosillos Mountains. To my northwest I could see the southeast realm of the Solotario Ring, a unique, symmetric ring of mountains eight miles across created by a giant lava bubble that burst a few million years ago. All that I could see of them though was their wind-eroded peaks. Salt Grass Draw ran just below the camp. To our north stood Hen Egg and Packsaddle Mountains, just barely visible in the morning brightness.

In the gathering heat and vivid sunshine, the surrounding desert took on a bleached-out, wasteland look after the green of South Carolina.

As I looked across the desert landscape, colors were subdued and pastel, except for a few purple blooms of sage and the occasional red flowers of small button cactus.

We set up a large main tent, and then an even larger canopy over it that included a sitting area extending off the front doorway. Strong Eagle explained this would help to make the tent cooler, creating a shaded area in front of it. We then put up three smaller tents. We finally had breakfast around noon. I was starving, even in the hot noon heat. Then it was rest time. We laid ourselves down and tried to sleep in the sweltering hotness.

Mid-afternoon, the hottest part of the day, Strong Eagle got ready to send us out to find our individual quest sites. He told us we must find our site and get back before nightfall. He instructed us to find a place that felt right to us for doing our quest. Before we ventured out, he counseled us about the dangers we needed to be aware of, both in our search for a quest site and during our quests.

"The desert is a *wild* place," he emphasized, "not hostile." He went on to explain that the desert was indifferent and unforgiving. It had no amenities for human creature comforts—no air conditioning, shelter, electricity (and all the things electricity provides), rest rooms, or Big Macs. It had rules, and if you did not play by those rules, you would pay a cost. He told us of tourists who came to visit the Big Bend area, not realizing how quickly the desert could become dangerous. "To survive in the desert, you must honor its truths." Strong Eagle told of his own scary experience of running out of water on a 112° F day. He could see heat waves radiating from his hands and arms. Having grown up in the desert, I was familiar with a lot of the things he was saying, so my mind began wandering.

For mystics and prophets, the desert has always been a place of mystery, renewal, and rebirth. It naturally creates a place for solitude, where life is stripped down to its bare essentials, its essence. In the desert, you let go of life's clutter and normal occupations; it becomes a place of nothingness or "no-thingness" in the Zen Buddhist tradition. As a result, this letting go or no-thingness becomes the birthplace of new or renewed "thingness."

In the Judeo-Christian tradition, the prophet Hosea spoke of the desert experience in some translations. Mystics Mechtild of Magdeburg and Meister Eckhart both used the image of the desert and its relation to nothingness and healing in their writings. The fourth-century Desert Fathers of Egypt lived their simple lives dedicated to Christ in the austerity of the desert.

Abraham, Jesus, Mohammed, and the Buddha all quested in the desert for a vision. Jesus went to the desert three times. The first was a vision quest of forty days. The number "40" is symbolic, with the four indicating sufficient time to do what needs to be done, and zero or the circle, an ancient symbol itself, meaning "to completion." There Jesus wrestled with questions about his ministry, his medicine work (in Native American terms), as symbolized by the temptations by Satan. In that life passage in the desert, the old Jesus died, and the Christ was born.

I thought about how the desert was for me both metaphor and real. It was the place of my "dark night of the soul," that is, a time for introspection and personal transition. But it was also a place where billions of stars, like angels, shone forth in brilliant, dazzling wonder. It was a place of loneliness, isolation, and solitude, but it had its own kind of beauty, both in darkness and light. It reminds us that to live fully in the light, we must be willing to spend time in the darkness.

The Big Bend desert has an abundance of clean air, sunshine, summer heat, winter cold, and its own special diversity of plant and animal life. Most of the latter are not your cute-and-cuddly sort. It was definitely a place most of us would find out of our comfort zone by its very nature. Its wildness resonated with a part of me at a deep level.

Big Bend is located in the Chihuahuan Desert, one of the four great deserts of the United States. I loved the Sonoran Desert with its large barrel and saguaro cacti. But the specific area where we were camping was the most rugged, wild, and beautiful desert I had ever seen. To really appreciate or experience the desert, you had to get out on it, live on it, survive on it, get truly away from civilization. That was what we would be doing for the four days of our quest, seven days altogether when you added in our first day after getting to base camp, another at the end to pack up and drive home, and travel to San Antonio.

My mind returned to Strong Eagle's discussion on the dangers and challenges before us. "It is a delicate land," he was counseling us. "The land we are on was once part of the Big Bend Ranch. Within a few decades, the Ranch's cattle had overgrazed the land of what little edible grass was available. Now all that is left is inedible cacti and brush, and not much brush at that. Slowly, ever so slowly, however, the land is healing itself." Strong Eagle pointed out the black fungus that was now growing in places. "It is rebuilding the soil," he said. He cautioned us, "Don't step on the flowers. Or fungus." Then he added, "'Flowers' means all the plants, not just the ones that are flowering or the purple sage that is blooming all around us."

My mind drifted back out as I thought about what I knew about the Big Bend desert. On the northern and eastern sides was shrub desert, which, as the name implies, is dominated by shrubs. It is characterized by mesquite, creosote, tarbush, and white-thorn acacia, with a smattering of the succulents, lechuguilla (New Mexico agave), and narrowleaf sotol. Shrub deserts occupy the lower elevations with deeper soil.[2] Shrub desert was where I had been during my Harley trip several years before. I had ridden my motorcycle from South Carolina to Big Bend. The Harley had broken down just outside of Lajitas, west of here.

We were now on the western side in what was known as a succulent desert, populated by succulents and semi-succulents that grow on the tops of slopes where large boulders rule. Cacti and blade-like lechuguilla plants dominated the area around us as well as this part of the desert in general. In addition to the common broad-leafed prickly pear cactus, there were a number of varieties of small barrel cactus species—button, clumps of hedgehog, star, and peyote (rare because of "overgrazing" by humans). Blooming purple sage plants were scattered about. I was amazed at the diversity of cacti in the area. I could hardly walk without stepping on one. I knew that there were over forty different species of these small cacti out here. So densely spaced were the small cacti and larger lechuguilla that walking around reminded me of being in a minefield.

Cacti fascinate me. They're a thorny issue, so to speak. We had several different kinds growing around our farm, and my office was filled with them. Mine were transplants, not native, of course. As a plant group, they have some interesting adaptations for living in the arid environments and the desert. They have their own special type of photosynthesis that is radically different from the rest of the plant kingdom. Plus, they breathe mainly at night when it's cool. Both of these adaptations help them conserve water.

Strong Eagle was very concerned about the flash floods, having nearly lost some of his last group in one. It was rainy season now in Big Bend, and the area could have some pretty spectacular flash floods. Having grown up in West Texas, I had firsthand knowledge of what he was talking about.

One of my most vivid memories as a child in Odessa was living on "Muskingum Draw." It was actually named Street, not Draw, but a draw was what the locals called it, and for very good reason. One dark, cold night, I watched with growing fright as flash flood rainwater lapped threateningly at our front door's threshold. The land is flat and there is no place for rainwater to go if it comes down too fast. We moved soon after that to another, higher-grounded house.

This early childhood experience was reinforced twice in my later years when I was a graduate student. The first instance was at the University of Texas at Austin, while I was working on a master's degree in zoology, studying fish populations. I was working under the famous ichthyologist, Professor Clark Hubbs. The first time we went out collecting fish, I noticed he would always turn the car around facing the road rather than the river. I asked him about it. He said it was in case of flash floods for a quick getaway, if needed. As a child of his even more famous ichthyologist father, Carl Hubbs, too many times they had had to make life-saving dashes to get out of massive waters rolling down the rivers toward them.

The second time, a few years later in the Davis Mountains not too far from here, I was collecting fruit flies (*Drosophila pseudoobscura*) that lived in the southwest, including the Big Bend area. The research was part of a large fifty-year study, plus it was my PhD dissertation research. I was here with my major professor from the University of Georgia in Athens. He and I had decided that, instead of camping out, we'd stay at the hotel above the campground at the state park where we were collecting. We later watched as campers below had their tents and gear washed down the river in a sudden flash flood, while they scrambled to the safety of the hotel. There had been no time for them to do anything but run for their lives. We were thankful not to have been among them.

Rainstorms on the desert can be impressive, not only because of the gully washers (flash flooding), but because of the lightning. When you are the tallest thing around, you're a ready-made lightening rod. Strong Eagle and Grandfather Chasing Thunder shared some real horror stories of people getting hit or almost hit by lightning out here. It did not reassure me of any sense of luck that I had had a great-grandfather struck and killed by lightning.

As I looked around at my fellow questees, Kelon, Ann, and Travis, I could see fear in their eyes. Strong Eagle's warnings were just what we wanted to hear as we were preparing to spend our time alone out in the desert. But Strong Eagle assured us that, out of the 180 or so vision questees he had taken out here, he had yet to lose one. My mother's voice came to me: "There's always a first time."

Strong Eagle then briefed us on the heat- and sun-related dangers—sunburn, dehydration, heat exhaustion, and heat stroke. He described their symptoms and how to prevent them and exposure. Exposure was caused during the summer months by sudden temperature drops from thunderstorms. It was not that it got that cold. Rather, the temperature dropped so suddenly, sometimes as much as 30 or more degrees, that you could rapidly become chilled. I had experienced such exposure conditions many times on motorcycle rides and on my first trip to Big Bend. On that trip, I had spent one night wrapped in an emergency space blanket after a big thunderstorm had rumbled through. I had brought only summer camping gear, and the thunderstorm had rolled in late in the night, dramatically dropping the temperature.

Then there were the critters, Strong Eagle warned. First, there were the potential bed and boot mates: most notable of which were scorpions and rattlesnakes. Both loved to crawl into bedrolls, and scorpions had a real proclivity for boots.

As legend and bragging had it, Texas scorpions were not your everyday sort of arachnid. At the end of my sophomore year in college, I worked on an oil field construction crew in the West Texas desert, running a jackhammer that weighed almost as much as I did. We would run across scorpions out there that were close to lobster size (well, maybe shrimp). Unlike their puny, pale brethren of the Eastern U.S., Texas scorpions are big, ugly, and have a vicious disposition to match. Although not usually fatal, their sting is nasty. When you are already stressed out with everything else during a quest, their painful sting could escalate psychologically to the unbearable, and panic could set in, which only increases the intensity of the pain.

There are also the scorpion's arachnid kin, the big hairy tarantulas that can get to be the size of your hand. Tarantulas are actually fairly harmless. They have a venomous bite, but you almost have to put your hand in their mouths. They are not exactly cute and cuddly, but they are relatively harmless. Their looks are worse than their bites.

Next on Strong Eagle's list came the rattlesnakes, coyotes, and mountain lions. Western rattlesnakes, interestingly enough, are smaller and less aggressive than their Eastern brethren. I couldn't see how anything larger than a jackrabbit could walk, much less run, on the dense desert minefield terrain. Their legs and feet would be shredded by all the sharp and cutting cacti and plants. So I figured (hoped and prayed), coyotes would not be a problem. What about mountain lions? Same as for coyotes I figured. Besides, the mountain lion was one of my totem archetypes. I did not cringe at the prospect of meeting up with a mountain lion, if it came to that—cautious, yes; fearful, well maybe.

Then there were biting bugs, including mosquitoes, Strong Eagle warned us. These, he said, come out at dusk and dawn mainly. There were mosquitos in Odessa, I remembered, but there was also water there. Mosquitos had to have water to hatch their eggs and grow their larvae. "Mosquitoes in the desert," I puzzled? But we had been attacked by mosquitoes early that morning, so, yeah, there were definitely mosquitoes out here.

Strong Eagle finished his talk. It was time to leave.

WHY WAS I DOING THIS?

As I walked back to get my gear, I asked myself again: now, why did I want to do this vision quest? I had spent a lot of time planning and thinking about it. Now that I was here standing on its threshold, self-doubt and anxiety were creeping in. Hell, they were running up screaming in my ear with each anticipated step.

I took a deep breath and thought to myself that the primary reason I came was about my spiritual journey. For me, everything else was organized around it. It was the center point of my *medicine wheel* or should I say, *medicine sphere*?

A SPIRITUAL JOURNEY

The medicine wheel is a sacred Native American (Plains Indians) symbol set out in the four cardinal directions: North, East, South, and West. Its center point symbolizes balance, wholeness, and health. If it is viewed in three dimensions as a sphere instead of a circle, then it can also represent Father Sky above and Mother Earth below.

Spirituality for me is about gaining inner peace and creating personal growth. It is not about religion, and certainly not some belief in some Big Guy in the sky, some supreme being that oversees Creation and all its workings. My personal spirituality has been an evolving mix of Zen Buddhism, Plains Indian spirituality, Stoicism, and science.

I reflected on the religion of my childhood and most of my adulthood, Christianity. I could no longer believe its myths, let alone its tenets. I no longer believed in a personal God. The closest I could get to God now was as a metaphor for the Laws of Nature and her processes, or underlying these, the ineffable, *Tao*.

Tao is a Chinese word for way, path, or route. Pronounced Dao, it is a holistic belief about the underlying nature of reality. It has no thingness: i.e., it is not a person, place, or thing; it is eternally nameless. Most of the teachings about Taoism that we are familiar with come from translations of the writings of Lao Tzu (551-479 B.C.E.).[3] The *Tao* can be discerned or experienced with our human intuition, but not defined. I am blessed in that I have experienced it. Not once, but several times.[4]

GROUNDED AND CENTERED

The second reason I came to this vision quest was to get better grounded and centered. I felt lost a lot of the time over the last few years, lacking both of these qualities.

Groundedness is the ability to be fully in your body and rooted to Mother Earth. The concept is symbolized by the Tree of Life, an archetypal symbol found in the teachings of many indigenous peoples, the Abrahamic traditions (Judaism, Christianity, and Islam), and others. When I am grounded, my roots are firmly anchored in Mother Earth, my arms and head reach into Father Sky, and my body is a thick, powerful trunk connecting the two. In his book *The Power of Now*, Eckhart Tolle says it means not being lost in your head with thoughts, thinking, or feelings, but rather being firmly in the now, in the present moment with what is going on.[5] It is a state of being in which we are whole, centered, and balanced within ourselves and our relationships. It is a deep, harmonious relationship with and knowing of our authentic selves. I had had a growing sense of not feeling well grounded for the last several years.

Being centered is about feeling a center point in your life that acts as a guide, a place to come back to when you are knocked on your keister by events in your life. On a Native American medicine wheel with its four directions, each direction can refer to part of you. North represents mind; South represents heart; East represents Spirit; and West represents the body. The center is where you want to be—at the balance of mind, body, spirit, and heart.[6]

MEDICINE WORK

Part of my ungroundedness had to do with my medicine work, my third reason for being on this vision quest. Medicine work is a Native American concept referring to healing and finding balance. In this case, it was my own and *mitakuye oyasin* medicine work, the latter being a Lakota term for "all my relations," essentially referring to all of the universe in its extended meaning. In Buddhist terms, my medicine work was about suffering, or rather ending it or at least reducing it. This is the core of Buddha's teachings. He taught about suffering: what caused it and how to end it.

As a professor of zoology, I didn't feel like I had been a very good scientist. I had good ideas and did some original research along with my students, but with the increased emphasis on research grants, the intense competition for funding, the tremendous struggle to publish our most innovative research, and its ultimate rejection by my scientific peers, I had found the university and research environment increasingly alienating. I was indeed suffering as I found an increasing discrepancy and discordance between why I had chosen the academic path and what that path had become.

After years of pouring everything I had into my research and career as a professor, it was burnout time, not too dissimilar to being out in a hot, dry desert without water! The day I received a rejection letter from the National Institutes of Health in which the reviewer wrote, "This is the best written grant proposal I have ever read. Too bad it will not be funded," I knew I was done. After much agonized thought, I threw in the towel at my next annual departmental review, handed my laboratory keys over to my department head and told him I wasn't going to do research anymore—the kiss of death in academia. I had written my last grant proposal. Closing that door led to a line of avenging efforts by the department head to "encourage" me to quit and give up my tenured position. In the end, I did quit, but on my terms, having gotten a degree in counseling and opened up my own private practice. Meanwhile, I had managed to get the large National Science Foundation grant that I controlled moved over to another college and out of his control.

Months after I had shut down my lab and research program and, in a casual conversation with my mother on our front porch on one of her rare visits from Texas, she said, "I don't know why you didn't go into mental health counseling. You were always so good at that." Aha!, a light bulb went off; yes, she was absolutely right—I was good at counseling and I enjoyed it. Duh, why hadn't I seen that?

As Jungian synchronicity would have it, a few days later I ran into a fellow Harley rider in the parking lot at the university. He had just finished earning his degree in counseling. What? I didn't even know my university offered a master's degree in counseling. I checked into it and found I could take courses for free as university faculty. I was accepted into the program and started my first class, just when my college's dean received funding from the National Science Foundation to establish a mentoring program for minority students in the sciences. They needed someone who was both a scientist and a therapist. Suddenly, I found myself running a minority program that required my background as both a scientist and my skills as a therapist. All was well, right?

Not quite. After setting up and running the program for a few years, I woke up one morning to find that the Board of Regents had done away with my College of Sciences. My department, which I was still in officially, was moved to another college. Before it was over, I had gotten locked into a confrontation with a new dean they had hired who wanted to change my program and job.

However, by now I had finished up my counseling degree, gotten my license (Licensed Professional Counselor), and even had an outside part-time practice going. At the same time, I had been getting training in advanced clinical hypnotherapy, and in the ancient fire walk exercise[7] such as we did during that training. That exercise is very much about courage and overcoming one's fears. The realization then came to me that it was time I fully left the university. I needed to have the courage to do it, and now I did. I realized that writing, teaching, and counseling were to become my medicine work.

The problem was, while this sounded good in theory, it did not work out so well in practice. Financially, I had not been successful. Having left my life at the university and its secure income, the reality of the entrepreneurial life was that I had not been able to make a living at doing my "medicine work." My family was about to go under financially. Did this mean I had been mistaken about my medicine work? This was one of the Big Questions I was out here to resolve.

INDIVIDUATION

Finally, the fourth reason I came to this vision quest was for my own inner personal growth—what Carl Jung called the individuation process.[8] Individuation is the integration process where one's personal and collective unconscious are brought into consciousness and assimilated into our whole personality. It is inner warrior work that takes courage. It means facing your demons. In my case, they were called Bandido and his dragon, Chaos, whom I will reveal shortly. And, little did I know, I was going to wrestle with these demons the whole four days!

FINDING MY QUEST SITE

I was the first to set out to find my quest site. Looking at the sun's position, I guessed it was now around 3:00 p.m. It had to be 95° F., at least. In my backpack were three gallons of water, weighing about 25 pounds total. That didn't sound like much, but with the high altitude, heat, and rugged country, combined with my no longer being a twenty-year-old, not to mention being in less than top physical shape, the water became heavy quickly. We were to leave the water at our quest site.

About 30 minutes into my walk, by my second arroyo, or draw, the 25 pounds of water was feeling very heavy. I descended into the draw and was huffing and puffing as I pulled myself up over the arroyo's wall. I spotted a small cave on the wall, but getting up to it would be difficult, and it was too small for me to sit up once there. Besides, Strong Eagle warned us about camping in draws, especially in light of the heavy rains and flash flooding the previous week.

I tried to keep walking mindfully and carefully, watching where I placed my feet on every step. This was what Strong Eagle refers to as "walking softly on the land." Here it was an enforced walking meditation, picking up my foot, gingerly putting my heal down, making sure there was nothing living under it, and then following with the rest of my foot, heel to toe. I checked my breathing, matching it with my steps: inhale, three steps; exhale, three steps. This did not last for long in the rugged terrain. Soon I was just trying to pay attention to where I placed my feet as I walked and breathed.

How do you know a place that resonates with you? That is what I was supposed to be looking for out here. It is about your energy and the land's energy that is in harmony with your own energy. I was well aware of what I was looking for, how it felt, but was overwhelmed by the intensity of my physical exertion and the heat. To sense such resonance, your mind has to be really clear, calm, and uncluttered with thoughts or emotions. Right now, my head was full of all kinds of thoughts running amok—and my anxiety was way on up there too. I paused and took some deep, calming breaths, pulling my thoughts back to just following my breath, letting the anxiety and heat just be there. Getting out of my head and back into my body and the now.

I recalled Carlos Castaneda's account of Don Juan trying to teach Castaneda how to find one of these resonant places.[9] Don Juan, in true Native American teaching fashion, let Castaneda wander around for hours trying to find somewhere out there in the desert where he felt a place that called out to him. Castaneda got very frustrated and angry with Don Juan. Don Juan didn't care. I felt much like Castaneda must have felt right now but told myself to keep looking and stumbled on. I was having great difficulty sensing the land's energy through the intense heat and my growing exhaustion. I felt overwhelmed by the heat radiating off the boulders and land around me, and the fiery sun bearing down on me as I walked.

I had some additional considerations too. I wanted a site that faced sunrise (northeast), gave me some protection from the harsh afternoon sun, and that allowed me to view the Chisos Mountains in the mornings. I wanted to be able to watch the sunrise each morning over the Chisos' peaks.

After a couple of hours of exhaustive looking, I gave up on the resonate idea and decided to just try to find a place that met my other requirements—and that minimally disturbed the cactus and lechuguilla plants that dominated the area.

Coming up out of another draw, I spotted an intriguing rock formation up ahead. It looked like a turtle walking on its hind legs. I was drawn to it. By this point, I had forgotten about Denise's reading about turtle medicine and the turtle bones I carried in my backpack.

Walking over to the rock formation, I turned and looked around. Nearby was a large boulder that sat atop the ridge and faced eastward. I walked over to it. Looking east, there stood the Chisos Mountains. Perfect for sunrise watching, I thought. The ground in front of the boulder, and where I was standing, was sparsely covered with vegetation. Only a couple of plants were in my way. The large boulder would be my backrest, providing protection from the hot western sun. I could throw my tarp over its top and have about three feet of headroom right up against it. A little taller would be better, but hey, beggars can't be choosers. Besides, I was tired of looking. I decided this was it. Taking off my backpack, I sat down in the shade of the boulder, looked around, and rested a while. Close to my boot was a small button cactus with a small red bloom beginning to barely peek out from its top. I was careful not to kick it.

I reached into my backpack and removed the bottles of water. They were wrapped in silver duct tape to help prevent breaks and leakage. This particular tape was very shiny. The last thing you wanted out here was to lose your water because of a puncture or break. In the bright desert sunshine, the shiny tape reflected the sunlight like a mirror.

Placing the water bottles in the shade of the large boulder, I stood and looked around again, surveying the surrounding landscape a little closer. It felt lonely and hostile to me. A moment of fear came over me about being out here for three very long days and nights. I said a short prayer asking for strength, courage, and blessings for what might lie ahead. This was warrior work, I thought. It would take courage. Hoisting my now empty backpack, I headed back to base camp to spend a last night.

2

LAJITAS LIZARD

Day 1 Early Morning

> Medicine Wheel direction: South
> Archetype: Healer (Turquoise Woman)
> Key words: lovingkindness, compassion
> Credo: Pay attention to what has heart and meaning[10]

WE AROSE AT DAWN, ROLLED UP OUR SLEEPING BAGS, AND ASSEMBLED our gear. Our mood was somber. I knew consternation must be showing on my face and in my body language. I could certainly see it in the faces of Kelon, Ann, and Travis.

Strong Eagle conducted a pipe ceremony to give us his blessing for our quests. The pipe ceremony was another of the seven sacred ceremonies of Native Americans. We sat in a circle on a blanket. The pipe was a traditional Native American one. It had a long, maybe 24-inch, handmade, hollowed stem. At the far end was a small bowl into which Strong Eagle packed tobacco. He lit the tobacco and did a blessing for the four directions. Interestingly, he did not pass the pipe around as had been done in other pipe ceremonies in which I had participated.

Afterwards, we threw on our backpacks. There was no breakfast, no juice, no coffee. Our time in the desert started officially last night. The four of us headed out in silence in separate directions to our individual quest sites.

As I head back to Turtle Rock, I passed Grandfather Chasing Thunder and said, "This feels heavy," meaning the quest, not my backpack. He took my meaning. With a somber expression, he remarked that a lot of powerful work would be done. I grimaced and kept walking. Although this was why I came, I admit that I was not looking forward to the next three days and nights.

It took me about an hour or so to reach my site. As I approached, Turtle Rock was easily visible. When I arrived, a small lizard was there waiting for me. He sat on a boulder looking at me as I walked up. Ahh, I thought, it's Lajitas. I smiled, and said to him, "Well, hello again, Lajitas." I had named him Lajitas Lizard from my earlier encounters with him. I had met Lajitas Lizard several times before. Well, not really him, but one of his relatives—relatively speaking. I laid my backpack down, leaning it against the large boulder that would serve as my backrest. He scuttled off. Well, so much for that, I thought.

I like lizards. Lizards seem to like me. Well, they like me as well as a reptile could, given their very limited brain. Lajitas was, I believed, of the checkered whiptail variety (species), though I was not a specialist in lizardology. He was small, about three inches long, with nondescript mottling of light brown, gray, and white that blended nicely with the rocks and surroundings.

The first time I met Lajitas Lizard was on my visit to Big Bend several years ago when my Harley had broken down just outside the town of Lajitas, Texas, not far from this vision quest location. I had managed to get the bike back to town, the engine coughing and spitting. I arranged for a tow truck, but the truck could not be there until the following day around noon. It was a 250-mile drive back to the nearest dealership, which happened to be in my old hometown of Odessa. They would have the parts I needed. When I woke up the next morning, I decided to take a hike up to the mountaintop on the nearby hiking trail. And there we met, my lizard friend and I, during that early morning hike, waiting for the tow truck.

Our second "meeting" was in Arizona. I was attending an advanced training in hypnotherapy. He "spoke" to me among a pile of polished stones with various animal totems carved into them. We had been instructed to choose a totem rock from a large pile of them. As I slowly passed my hand over the stones with my eyes shut, I could feel energy emanating from one of the stones. Still with closed eyes, I picked it up. When I opened my eyes there was the carving of a lizard etched into the stone. He sits on my altar at home now to remind me of lizard medicine.

Lizard medicine in Native American lore is about the shadow side of reality. This could be the place of dreams before they are manifested as our fears, hopes, or the things we are resisting. Lizard reminds us to pay attention to our dreams and notice if our future is coming up behind us. He is a walker of the dream time. Ancient and deeply connected to Mother Earth, the wisdom of his genes stretches back to a time before humans, even before any mammals walked the earth. Lizard carries a reptilian brain. As humans we all have relics of that reptilian brain. It comes into play at the most fundamental level of survival and reproduction. I would be using the reptilian part of my human brain out here in the desert the next few days—just trying to survive this ordeal!

Neurobiologist Paul MacLean divided the vertebrate brain into the reptilian brain, the paleomammalian brain, and the neomammalian brain in terms of its evolution.[11] The reptilian brain is the most primitive, consisting of primarily the lower brain centers. (Sorry, Lajitas.) The paleomammalian brain added to the reptilian brain a larger cortex and the limbic system with its greater emotional repertoire. The neo-mammalian brain added to these our complex cerebral hemispheres that enable our higher cognitive functioning.

I began a ceremony to ask the land for permission to quest there, introducing myself to its rocks, plants, and critters. My intentions, I stated, were not to harm, but to ask for their wisdom. I would try to walk softly while I was here. I walked around the area dropping pinches of tobacco on the ground as an offering for permission and help.

I had to move a lechuguilla plant and asked its permission. I was not careful as I dug it up, and one sharp leaf impaled my left calf. I guessed that was a No? The cut was not very deep, but blood dripped from the quarter-inch long wound. A blood offering to the land, I thought. I transplanted the plant to another spot, and watered it with my urine, hoping it appreciated the gesture of water in this dry, dry land.

It was a clear day and the sand's heat was rapidly beginning to build. To my east, in the far distance, out over the Chisos Mountains, the sun was up above the mountains now. As the sun rose, the wind blew stronger. A few white, fluffy clouds could be seen on the far horizon. The sky above was huge and blue. A pollution haze hung over the Chisos Mountains, the morning sun making the haze glow an unhealthy grayish orange. Yuk! The air pollution came from a large coal-burning power plant across the border in Mexico. Its pollution carried far and wide over the southwest, bunching up around mountain ranges.

Next, I set up a tarp for shade and protection should it rain. I threw my 5' x 10' blue tarp over the top of the large boulder. Tying lead lines to the end grommets, I anchored them over the boulder's top to large rocks that were behind and to its side. Strong Eagle had shown us how to tie special adjustable tension knots to use in the high wind, but I found the cord I had brought slipped too easily and had to improvise another way to tie the lines.

As I worked, a strong gust of wind whipped the tarp around, threatening to tear it away from me. I gathered bigger rocks to help hold the lead lines and placed rocks on the untied portion of the tarp to hold it while I worked on the end that would be my "high end." Under it I could sit with my back against the large boulder.

I moved to the other end, the "low end." This end of the tarp was more problematic. There was nothing strong enough or tall enough to support it, especially in the high wind. Strong Eagle had had each of us buy two 3-foot long dowel rods at the Walmart in Del Rio to use to help support our tarps. I went to my backpack and pulled these out. We had already driven nails in one end of the dowels back in the Walmart parking lot, leaving about an inch of the nail with its head sticking up out of the rods. I looped the grommet of my tarp over the nail, then tied a lead line to the nail. The nail head held the tarp on the rod as well as gave a place to tie the lead line. The other end of the lead line I anchored to small boulders, piling extra boulders around for added weight. I was sweating by now and paused for a moment to change out of my blue jeans into shorts before moving on to fix the second support rod. Lajitas Lizard stuck his head up from beneath a rock beside me. I commented to him that he could help a little instead of just standing there. He scurried off, chuckling.

At my quest area, I demarcated a crude circle by placing stones around my tarp. The circle was roughly 12 feet in diameter, with the tarp as the center. This would be my space for the next three days. I would stay inside this circle, except to take care of bodily necessities and a daily check-in walk down to a pre-arranged altar site so Strong Eagle would know I was still alive. I decided to use my urine to mark my territory. This would theoretically help discourage potentially dangerous predators from entering my circle.

Strong Eagle said we were to take special care to open and close the circle when we left and entered so that nothing unwanted came in. I placed prayer ties on bushes in the four directions and prayed for the wisdom of each direction. The ties were small squares of colored cotton material in the Lakota colors with a pinch of tobacco in each and tied with cotton thread.

Toward the east, I placed a small yellow prayer tie pouch, tying it on one of the bushes and asked for the vision of the eagle so that I might see far to the place where my path needed to go. East is also the direction of rebirth and a new day, so I prayed for rebirth and clarity. The eagle is also a symbol for Spirit.

Toward the south, I placed a green prayer tie pouch and asked that I might carefully listen to my heart as it spoke during my quest, and that I might hold myself and this experience with compassion.

To the west, I placed a black prayer tie pouch. This symbolized the dark night of my soul. I asked black bear, its totem, to help me see what I needed to see inside. I recalled drawing his medicine card in my sitting with Denise, Strong Eagle's wife. I asked to see clearly the things about myself that it was time to let go of and those parts of me I needed to nurture more. Finally, to the north, I placed a white prayer tie pouch. North is the direction of wisdom, of the Teacher.

I used sage and rosemary to smudge and bless and purify my circle, the idea being that the aromatic smoke from the herbs and plants is purifying. In my sitting area at home, I use sage to "purify" my area before meditating. It is not, of course, that smudging really purifies. Rather, it helps you get your mind in the right psychological place. It is an olfaction (smell) cue for the brain. Olfaction is tightly associated with the limbic system and its emotions. Many religious ceremonies and practices routinely use incense and plant aromatics for smudging to the same purpose.

According to Strong Eagle, inside the circle we were safe—as long as we didn't ask or let anything into it. (I would soon find out this did not apply to mosquitoes and biting flies.) Strong Eagle had warned us that if we were approached by an animal or a spirit, to ask it three questions before deciding to let it enter: what was its name, what was its purpose, and who sent it? I did not take this lightly, having had an encounter with an angry Anasazi warrior spirit on my first vision quest in New Mexico. That was scary and intense.

The sun was now well up in the mid-morning sky and scorching hot by the time I crawled under my tarp. I smudged the area under the tarp with sage and sprinkled rosemary water around, again asking for blessings. "Now what?" My quest had begun in earnest. I sat there for a few minutes. My chigger bites, God bless them, started to itch. I scratched at them, which only made them itch more as histamines were released from the inflamed tissues. I remembered the anti-itch cream I had picked up in Del Rio and applied it.

While waiting for the itching to subside, I closed my eyes and tried to sense/feel the energy and spirit of the land around me. At one level, all I seemed to be aware of were the waves of intense heat emanating off the mountain and rocks around me. On another level, I could feel Lajitas Lizard watching me. I said a little prayer asking the itching to stop, figuring it wouldn't hurt to ask.

Looking eastward, I could see the Chisos Mountains at the heart of Big Bend National Park. They stood shimmering in the morning's gathering heat, making them look almost like a mirage lying in the distance. The imagery came to me of a guru sitting up there looking down on me. He sat on his high mountain of spiritual evolution looking down at my futile attempts to climb to a higher spiritual mountain myself—to reach a higher plane of spiritual evolution. That was the real heart of what I was doing out here, why I did these intense experiences such as vision quests and Zen sesshins. I wanted the greater sense of inner peace and personal growth this evolution heralded.

As the morning progressed, the minutes and the heat crawled turtle-slow toward the afternoon. Mother Wind blessedly brought cooling gusts.

I reached out with my mind again to touch the spirit and energy of the desert around me. Again, all I could really sense was the intense heat. It was overwhelming, dominating, excruciating. It reminded me of the sweat lodge. Right now, my world was governed by heat and itching. Not a good omen for the next three days. My anxiety was really coming up. I asked myself, how could baking in this desert oven possibly be spiritually enriching? Trying to step away from my anxiety, I focused on my breath, attempting to bring myself back to a state of *mindfulness*.

Mindfulness is about maintaining a moment-to-moment awareness of our body, thoughts, feelings, and the environment around us. At the same time, it is about accepting, without judging, all of these as they are in the moment. It is about not separating oneself from all of these, of being non-dualistic.

Dualism is about separation and goes back to the mind-body split of French philosopher, Rene Descartes (1596 – 1650), in what is referred to as the Cartesian worldview. Descartes was the inventor of the Cartesian coordinate system and analytical geometry, and one of the founders of the scientific revolution; he argued most elegantly from this perspective. His famous statement, "I think, therefore I am" separated subject from object. There were those things that "think," the subject, and those things thought about, the objects.

Theologian Matthew Fox argued that the original sin in Augustinian Christianity was not that humankind was basically evil, but rather that our sin was to view ourselves as separate from nature and each other[12]—to perceive that we were *not* interconnected. Metaphorically, Adam and Eve were kicked out of the Garden of Eden because they held themselves as separate from and not part of nature. This is the sin of duality.

At that point in my reflection, Lajitas hopped back upon his rock. Looking at him, I said, "Out here, Lajitas, I certainly feel part of nature.

I can't get away from it no matter where I turn or hide." He bobbed his head up and down as if agreeing with me. Out here I had an opportunity to experience non-duality raw and unedited.

Dualism is the mainstay of science, with the exception of quantum mechanics perhaps. Many scientists go so far as to claim that mind does not really exist, much less spirit. Mind, consciousness, and especially spirit, are inconvenient concepts to science. Humankind's self-reflective consciousness or mind was an anomaly, best ignored.

Dualism led to a mechanistic worldview that sees matter assembled into separate, independent, interacting units, similar to pool balls on a pool table. Hence, the concept of the atom was originally thought of as an indivisible unit of matter. The integrity of these units of matter was unchanged by their interactions with other matter. The pool balls bounce against each other unchanged in their internal integrity.

This mind-matter, dualistic worldview was in contrast to the mystic worldview, which was a unitary worldview that preceded Cartesian duality. Mysticism is a common thread of many indigenous philosophies, such as the Eastern traditions of Buddhism, Hinduism, and Taoism as well as Jewish Kabalistic, Christian mystics, Native American spirituality, and Celtic folklore. Today it is hinted at in quantum physics.[13] This mystic worldview sees everything in the universe as interconnected. Hence, electrons became not little planet-like structures orbiting around a nucleus, but rather energy fields with probability distributions of when they will be at a certain location or where they will be. (Albert Einstein, the father of the atomic age, hated quantum mechanics. It gave too "messy" a picture of the universe, not to mention being too complex.) In this worldview, you must love your neighbor as yourself because he or she is part of you. Everything you do affects everyone and everything else in the universe. Pool balls colliding are changed.

Lajitas Lizard was still there, not saying anything. Lizards could be like that. I continued my thoughts out loud, talking to him: "More enlightened Christianity has incorporated this unitary worldview in terms of *panentheism*. Panentheism means, literally, everything in God. This is to be distinguished from *pantheism*, Lajitas, which meant everything *is* God, or many gods." Lajitas looked at me, I looked at him. We were silent. With that, he scurried off, perhaps bored with the conversation. I continued my thoughts in silence.

Nature, through this desert experience, would help me understand my interconnectedness, to experience it directly. As said during many Native American ceremonies, the Lakota phrase *mitakuye oyasin* means "all my relations" and is an acknowledgement of our universal interconnectedness. We are all related, not only all humans, but animals, plants, rocks, water, animate and inanimate objects. We are our brother's (and sister's) keepers. Our "neighbors," as in "love thy neighbor," include all of creation, not just the people living near us. We are all interdependent on each other.

It is along this same vein that when Jesus was asked by the Pharisees which was the greatest commandment, his reply was to love God above all else, and, likewise flowing from this first commandment, to love others as ourselves.

By late morning, the heat was on broil. I stripped down to just my cutoffs. My brilliantly white (as in pale) skin was in sharp contrast to the desert's gray and brown rocks around me. I was more than thankful for the cooling gusts of wind, some of which were very strong and threatened to blow away my flimsy tarp.

A roadrunner (*Geococcyx californicus*), also called a chaparral, suddenly flitted down a few feet away. He looked me over. "Where did you come from, my friend?" I asked. Images of the roadrunner cartoon and Wile E. Coyote came to me. Walking right up to the edge of my circle, he stood there eyeing me, as if saying, "What are you doing here, fool?" They are such a brazen species. As instructed by Strong Eagle, I asked, "Who are you?" His answer came back, "*Who* are you?" He flew off. (Roadrunners can be very cynical birds—and rude.)

I recalled my last encounter with a roadrunner. It too was right here in Big Bend. I was setting up camp at the Chisos Mountain campground and just as I started clearing a spot to place my tent, a roadrunner flew down and started slowly walking around the area looking for food. Never mind that I was standing right there, prepared to throw my ground cloth down. He completely ignored me, pecking here, pecking there. I rolled my ground cloth back up, sat down under the picnic canopy in the shade, and waited for him to finish. After about five minutes, he flew off, over to the next campsite. No thank-you's, not a word.

In answer to the roadrunner's question, a strong gust of wind shook my tarp, dislodging one corner from its upright rod. I got up and re-affixed it. Crawling back under my tarp, I asked the wind, "So, OK, who am I?" No reply. It was worth a try.

Hunger and fatigue were setting in. I took a drink of water, carefully wet my t-shirt and bandana, and place them over me. Their wetness made the wind feel like an air-conditioned breeze. I sighed with the wonderful coolness it generated. It reminded me of evaporative coolers we used when I was growing up in Odessa. I dozed off.

Later, in the heat of the morning, as I reached to take another drink of water from my first gallon milk jug, my attention was brought to the pendant around my neck. It was a two-dimensional, disc-shaped silver pendant, tarnished by years of wear and sweat. I had worn it for years as a symbol of my spiritual journey and had come across it in a vendor's booth down in Manzanillo, Mexico, on one of my advanced hypnotherapy trainings. I reached up and slipped it off over my head. Its leather strap broke as I pulled on it.

Holding the pendant in my hand, I was reminded of the mystery and meaning it symbolized for me right then in my journey. The shape was a stylized Celtic cross with a spiral in its middle. Very similar in meaning to the Native American medicine wheel. The cross resembled a plus sign, all of its arms being the same length. As such, their equal lengths delineated a circle on their outside. The large arms were covered with minute, intricate Celtic knot designs. This cross had numerous meanings for me.

In terms of spiritual and personal growth, the horizontal arms of the cross symbolized unfolding in the personal dimension. One arm stood for our inward journey of insight and transparency of our inner self. The other arm symbolized our growth in interpersonal relationships—interconnectedness with each other. The vertical axis of the cross was about our spiritual unfolding where our feet are grounded in the earth, our genes, and natural processes, as we are creatures of these. Toward the sky, the top of the cross pointed to our place in and interconnectedness to the cosmos.

The arms and legs of the cross also symbolized for me the four sacred constellations in my life: the cardinal directions, north, south, west, and east; the four elements of the Celts and ancient medieval science—earth, water, wind, and fire; the four traditions that had so influenced my life—Judeo-Christianity, Native American spirituality, Buddhism, and science; the four forces of quantum physics—electromagnetism, gravity, strong nuclear, and weak nuclear forces; and the four forces that drive the evolutionary process—natural selection, mutation, migration, and random genetic drift.

The cross formed a circle, which was a symbol for completeness or wholeness. A circle is one of the five archetypal symbols identified by Carl Jung—circle, square, cross, spiral, and triangle.[14]

The spiral on the pendant had layered meanings for me also. A spiral is an ancient symbol. For me, it symbolized my spiritual journey. It also stood for the DNA double helix, itself an ancient symbol found in many ancient cultures. Sometimes drawn as two entwined snakes, the DNA double helix reminded me of my long heritage and connection to the rest of life on Mother Earth. Finally, the spiral was also a symbol of a shamanic door. The doorway for those who can and dare enter into the right-brain world of "spirit." It was the spiral, our life's journey, that took us to the center, our True Self.

Looking up from underneath my tarp, toward the clear, vast blue sky above, I saw a hawk circling high in the air. I knew that beyond the hawk were the stars and cosmos, or heavens, as the ancients would say.

Lajitas Lizard paid me another visit. Again, he didn't say anything, just looked. He was a lizard of few words. His looking reminded me that was what I was doing: looking. A vision quest is about having a vision; about taking an unflinching look at yourself and your life. About finding your truth.

It is a death/rebirth process, taking advantage of a natural creative process. You step outside of the clutter and conditions of your life to take an unwavering look at yourself in order to find yourself or to be more authentic or real. You sever your ties with your old life for a few days to find a new life, a clearer perspective on your old life, or both. You might have a vision or a visit of the spirits, but these are outside of yourself. What you are looking for is inside. You isolate yourself so that you can find yourself. You are not out there to "find God." The irony is that if you find yourself, you would also find God. This is part of the Great Mystery.

Metaphorically, a vision quest is a time of death and then rebirth. Death is a time of nothingness, of not existing. There is no old self. There is no new self. There is just no-selfness. We are undefined. It is a time of chaos. During the quest, we are asked to be undifferentiated embryonic cells floating in our mother's womb. In this case, mother was Mother Earth. Here in the desert, I drifted in this undefinedness, this chaos.

During the quest, we are to let go of the things in our lives that no longer serve us. It is a time to let them die. I had written mine on small pieces of paper to be burned in a ceremony here at my quest site as a symbolic way of letting go. Since my childhood, I wanted to let go of my anxiety, loneliness, shame, and desire for approval. Then there were the life transitions that I wanted to make peace with: Carol, my wife, and I getting older; our children growing up; becoming grandparents. (Crossing my mind suddenly were my membership in AARP, along with senior discounts.)

During this quest, I would realize that these things I wanted to let go of and make peace with were not my enemies. Rather, they were some of the great teachers of my life. (Well, maybe not the AARP and senior discounts.) I had learned their lessons, and it was time to move on. So, I would thank them for their teachings and make peace with them instead. All these letting-go's were little deaths in our lives, in preparation for the Big Death at the end.

Many shamanic traditions involve a death experience, some not so little. The lightning shamans of Peru were examples. Part of shamanic training could involve near death experiences. "Shamans" are born from these experiences. As Strong Eagle's words about lightning came back to me, I hoped not to have one of these experiences out here on my quest.

Lajitas Lizard was still there on his rock watching me. He asked if I was afraid. (Well, maybe he didn't actually say anything, but I could see he was thinking it.) "Yes," I answered, "I'm afraid." I paused, thinking, remembering the recent birth of my youngest grandson, Brandon, and continued, "Imagine the sheer terror of the newborn coming out of the safe, warm, all-encompassing womb into the alien, unknown world outside." Brandon had come out of his mother and had to spend a couple of days in an incubator, because his lungs were not quite as developed as they needed to be. Any birth process was scary, including rebirth. "Yes, Lajitas, I am scared."

Because this process is so frightening and stressful, most people, I think, try to avoid it. They attempt to move laterally in their lives as opposed to going deeper inside. A vision quest is about going deeper, becoming a fuller, more authentic you. With lateral movement, you try to change the world outside of you. You change jobs because you don't like your work or boss or pay. You buy another house because the current one doesn't suit you. You buy more things, fill your life with stuff. Or you change relationships.

For most people in our culture, they feel it is easier to change relationships than to stick it out and work on the ones they are in. So, they jump to a new relationship, or out of an old one and just hope for a new one to come along, the sooner the better. A lot of my clients in counseling fit this pattern. They think changing their outside world will bring them happiness. They think the outside world is the problem—that *others* are their problem. However, no matter where they go, there they are: their issues are still with them. Working on issues requires going deeper within our self, not wider outside our self. We have to be willing to let go and let the old parts of us die so that new parts can be born.

Following the death of these old parts comes rebirth. In our lives, we go through many little deaths and rebirths. Some of these are heavier than others. With each, there is a grief process that must be worked through. This is how we grow. Rebirth is about a new you being born into the world. Like Christianity's archetypal resurrection story, it is replayed in each of us as we go through our lives. Life is a continuous replay of this dynamic circle of death/rebirth so we can grow and become more fully human.

This natural creative death/rebirth, circular process is also a fractal that is replayed throughout creation as creation itself evolves and changes. The process is reflected from the level of the gene, to the body, to the mind, to everywhere in nature. It is integral to evolution itself, to biological development, and to personal and spiritual growth. In the arts, it is replayed in the epic hero's journey, in our mythology, and in our theology (same thing). It is found in our daily lives on a less dramatic scale as we go through the creative processes inherent in meeting the challenges of everyday living. It is even reflected in the human sexual stages of excitement, plateau, orgasm, and resolution.[15]

According to Strong Eagle, a vision quest is a replay of this death/rebirth cycle. It can be divided into four stages of a four-directional, dynamic circle. The first stage is preparation. Preparation is a time of just living. During this stage, we are collecting data about our life. Things are fine for a while, then we start getting bored, events from outside our lives change, and we start to realize we have become or are becoming dissatisfied with our lives. Or things are not going well, and we finally get to a point where we want to, or feel we have to, make changes in our life.

As a prelude to a quest, there is a growing need for clarity, a new vision (truth) of one's life, or a need to let go of things that no longer benefit us. The end result of this stage is an increasing pressure to commit to making meaningful changes.

In my own life, my preparation stage for this quest started after I left the university where I had been teaching for 23 years, relinquishing my tenured professor position and its relatively comfortable salary. I also gave up my counseling practice and doing workshops and seminars, all of which had failed financially. Over and over they failed. Nothing I tried seemed to work, or rather, worked well enough. Twice during that period, I nearly went bankrupt. I began to doubt my abilities and my calling to my medicine. I felt increasingly frustrated and angry. Depression set in. I was lost. The stress was overwhelming.

Stage two of the creative rebirthing process can be called the separation stage. A threshold is passed, and we feel a need to separate ourselves from our everyday lives for a while to gain perspective. For couples in a relationship, this may be a time of separation, either emotionally and/or physically. In the quest, Strong Eagle calls this stage severance. We start severing connections to our everyday lives in preparation for going on our quest. Stage two began for me when Strong Eagle emailed me about doing this quest, and I agreed and committed to doing it.

My severance stage, with Strong Eagle's coaching, involved time spent out in nature. I used a sweat lodge a group of us had built out in the forest on our small farm in preparation for a workshop Strong Eagle was coming out to South Carolina to do. That had been months ago but it was still standing. Every day, I tried to spend time out there by myself, usually with Princess, my faithful friend and dog. I looked at my life, where I was, and where I wanted to go. I asked questions about what had worked and what had not, and why. I journaled a lot. I made a list of what I wanted to let go of on my quest. My final separation came as I boarded the plane to fly to this quest.

Stage three, for me, was this time out in the desert or wilderness. This third stage is the time of death of the old, of chaos when we are still undefined and not yet reborn. It is the dark night of the soul. This is a critical period because it is a time for great insight and reorganization. New life emerges from out of the chaos. Creation is replayed. And here I sat.

I was awaiting the fourth and final stage, which is that of incorporation or rebirth. We come out of our desert with new perspectives, new insights, new visions about who we are and where our path is to go from there—or that is the theory at least. Maybe it is the same path, but with new understanding about ourselves and others in our lives.

Life as a spiritual journey is a replay of this death/rebirth cycle. If we are to grow spiritually and personally, that journey consists of ongoing replays of this creative cycle. One way or the other, we each must spend time out in our own desert. Either we head out voluntarily, as Christ and Buddha did, or life eventually throws us out there kicking and screaming. I had walked out into the desert voluntarily.

3

TURQUOISE WOMAN

DAY 1 AFTERNOON

AROUND ME A FEW OF THE CACTI AND PURPLE SAGE WERE JUST beginning to bud out; their slight colors beginning to peek out from their protective petals. The rains a few days ago were enough to kick them into flowering. I wondered if they would blossom while I was out here.

By afternoon, I had realized I was sunburned! Shit! Despite the tarp I was under, enough of the sun's UV rays had penetrated to burn me. "Wonderful," I said out loud. Fortunately, it was usually fairly easy for me to shut off the discomfort of sunburns. It was a mental trick I had learned as a kid because I sunburned so easily with my fair skin. But beyond coping with the pain, I would need to prevent further burning. What could I do out here right now? Wearing more clothes would not do in the heat. I looked at my sheet folded up beside me. An idea! I unfolded the sheet and tied it up right beneath the tarp as a second sunscreen layer. It lowered my headroom but gave me more shade.

A gust of wind whipped the tarp, and my hat, which had been sitting beside me because the tarp was now too low for me to wear it, was blown over on its side. And there, clinging to the side of my hat, was a picture of a golden retriever given to me by Strong Eagle's youngest daughter. A stab of loneliness hit me. I missed my family and my ever-constant companion, my golden retriever, Princess, who along with my two grandchildren, ages five and eight, were my *spiritual* advisors. More like spiritual reminders. The wisdom of children and pets—they have been some of my most profound teachers. I thought about Turquoise Woman, another of my spiritual advisors. I had not felt her presence so far in this adventure. Hmm.

Turquoise Woman is my archetype for the South and the Healer. She is also my symbol for Mother Nature and my anima, what Jung called our ideal or enigmatic female. A shaman would say that she is one of my spirit guides.

Archetypes are important for both our spiritual[16] and personal growth.[17] Mostly, we are usually unaware of their roles in our lives as they play out in our brain's neural circuitry at the subconscious level. However, they can be made conscious and used to help guide us in our life decisions, purpose, and challenges. Over many past years, I had often consulted with Turquoise Woman on problems or issues when I needed clarity, trying to see things from her perspective, in the same way I consulted with my other archetypes.

Navaho mythology speaks of Turquoise Woman, along with her sister, White Shell Woman.[18] The two sisters were the daughters of First Man and First Woman. Instead of the first-borne brothers, Cain and Able, of the Hebrew/Genesis myth where Cain slays Able, these first-borne sisters were heroes. Turquoise Woman is also known as Changing Woman to the Apache. It was in this capacity, changing, that she resonated with me. Well, she was also very feminine, and that part got my attention, too.

As Changing Woman, she embodies the cycles and processes of nature. "Cycles" include such things as the four seasons, the circadian sleep-wake cycle, the menstrual cycle, the tidal cycle, the moon's cycle, the cycle of cell division, DNA replication, etc. "Processes" include biological evolution, chaos and self-organization, development, Jung's individuation, and others.

As the heat and the afternoon hours passed, now that I was settled in and "officially" into my quest, I felt my anxiety and loneliness coming up. I wanted to know if Turquoise Woman had any insights or advice for me for my quest. Her answer was not immediately forthcoming.

The sun was down a little on the horizon now, but the wind had picked up. I figured it was probably around 4:00. It had to be above 95 degrees. Under my tarp, I leaned back against my boulder backrest and decided if Turquoise Woman would not come to me, I would go to her. I closed my eyes and touched the tip of my thumb and index finger on my right hand together.

This touching together of these fingers is what's known in hypnotherapy as an anchor—a physical action or artifact that facilitates a mental shift. In this case, it helped me shift to an alternate state of consciousness, from left brain (cerebral cortex) dominance to right brain dominance, and activated my parasympathetic nervous system, calming me. After a few breaths, I had made the mind shift, and found myself in my unique power place in my mind.

My power place was actually right here in Big Bend, as it turned out. I had "found" it on one of my earlier shamanic journeys and had recognized it years later, when I came across some pictures of it in a collection of postcards sold in a packet at the Big Bend Park's store. I had never been to my power place in body, only in spirit. It sat high in the mountains of Mariscal Canyon overlooking the Rio Grande river far below. It was usually night when I was there, my spirit's choice, with a sky filled with brilliant stars and a moon so full and bright I could read by it.

Transported there in spirit again now, I was sitting on a Native American blanket on the ground. Behind me was an old twisted cedar tree. In front of me was a blazing fire. But this fire was no ordinary fire. It burned white hot, translucent.

I stepped into the fire, standing at its center. It first burned away my clothing. There was no pain as it worked its way from my feet up my legs, hips, genitals, waist, abdomen, chest and back, arms, neck, and finally my head. As it burned, it burned away an outer crust that fell off. It was burning away attachment, attachment to ego, to pain, hurts, wants, desire—the clutter and detrital slag of my life. The things in my life that created suffering. It was a purifying fire. Underneath, my body was shining now with its own translucent light. I stepped out of the fire in this luminous, light body. Sitting back down on my blanket, I heard footsteps behind me and turned.

Turquoise Woman was coming toward me. I watched her approach. As usual she was dressed in a white deerskin dress. Around her neck was a turquoise necklace and in her long dark hair, holding it back, was a turquoise comb of some sort. When she was a few feet from me, our eyes met and I heard her say, "Hello, Love." It was not so much that I actually heard her, as felt her words. I stood as she neared.

She walked up to me, standing close. I could smell her scent. It was like spring air, laced with a rich, deep, organic earthiness and sexuality. Like lush dark soil, moist and fertile. Her skin was dark and glowed with its own golden light. After a few seconds, she started humming then moving and pulling me around the fire in a slow dancing motion in time with her tune. I was taken off guard. She had never danced with me before. For several minutes we danced around the fire.

Then she stopped, took my hand and placed it on her chest over her heart and placed her hand over my heart. I could feel her chest rising and falling as she breathed. I could feel the softness of her breast.

She stepped back, aging before my eyes, going from a body of a 20-year old, to an older woman, growing older with each passing second, and finally to that of an old woman. Her smile never faded. Her eyes continued to sparkle. I didn't panic. I had seen this before. She was, after all, Changing Woman. Then she metamorphosed back to her 20-year-old self. In my head I heard her voice, "I cannot help you, but I will be here. This is a journey you must take by yourself," an enigmatic smile appeared on her lips, and then she was gone.

I emerged from my trance back into the desert daytime and heat, saddened to be alone once again, and wondering what her smile meant, what the dancing was all about. Did she know something I didn't know about what was to come? Probably. Oh, great, I thought.

At this point, Lajitas popped back up on his rock next to me. He looked at me and then in the direction Turquoise Woman had last been standing, then back to me, as if he had seen her and was asking where she had gone. I went on to explain to him.

"Lajitas, we each have an ideal prototypal, innate image. For men, this image is female, which Jung called our *anima*; women have an ideal male or *animus* image.[19] Consciously, we may not be able to see this image, but when a member of the opposite sex with some of those ideal characteristics pops into our lives, we instantly know it, and are drawn to that person. Evolutionarily this is thought to be directly related to reproduction and hence the survival of our genes. I assume homosexuality flips this to an 'ideal other'?" At that point, Lajitas lost interest I guess, and scurried off. You would think a lizard would be interested in things about reproduction and mating. I continued my thoughts to myself in silence, as a really strong blast of hot wind again rattled my tarp, causing it to flap wildly.

All of this anima stuff is important in terms of whom we choose to mate with and stay with in long-term relationships. Research has shown that when choosing a mate, we are attracted to those individuals that show signs of wellbeing and fitness.[20] For example, the symmetry of the body's left and right sides indicates a potentially healthy mate choice. Asymmetry indicates the opposite.

We are generally attracted to non-kin related people, as this is an evolutionary mechanism to avoid *inbreeding*. Inbreeding is the mating between closely related individuals. Inbreeding results in the expression of deleterious genes that lowers our evolutionary fitness, that is the survival and reproduction of our offspring. We all carry deleterious genes, but most are masked by healthy genes. Kin are more likely to carry the same deleterious genes we do, as related individuals share many of the same genes. If we mate and have offspring with other individuals who carry those same deleterious genes, those genes are unmasked, and our offspring may suffer in terms of their survival and reproduction.

Familiarity overrides our basic biological drive to mate. This means that children reared together from an early age are usually not attracted to each other sexually, even if they are genetically unrelated. You can see this same phenomenon in other animals. For example, puppies that are reared together will not usually try to mate with each other, even if from different parents. This avoids inbreeding and promotes outbreeding, i.e., mating between unrelated individuals.

Our anima and animus play a role in this evolutionary strategy—avoiding inbreeding. For example, for men, our individual anima is not going to look like our sister or mother; a woman's animus will not resemble her brother or father. Such imagery also plays a role in long-term pair bonding, not only short-term sexual behavior. Long-term pair bonding is associated with health and wellbeing when a long-term relationship is secure and enduring.

Turquoise Woman is what psychologist Carl Jung referred to as an *archetype*, but exactly what is an archetype? His conception of archetypes was very Platonic, in that archetypes represented an *ideal* type. His formulation, however, predated our modern understanding of genes and neurobiology. What do we know now about archetypes in terms of these? More importantly, perhaps, are archetypes real or just part of our imagination?

In Zen-speak, like a koan,[21] the answer is, yes. They are both real *and* part of our imagination. Real, in that they are part of our species' survival heritage. Part of our imagination, in that we personalize them, especially if they get to the consciousness level or appear to us in our dreams or other altered states of consciousness. The archetypes are individualized for each individual, based on background, life experiences, and perhaps the specific genes the individual has. But what exactly are archetypes? To begin to answer that question we will need to turn back to Jung, and his ideas on personality.

Jung distinguished three levels of personality: ego, personal unconscious, and the collective unconscious. Archetypes, he noted, were part of our collective unconscious. Jung envisioned the Collective Unconscious as a species' trait and therefore inherited. Archetypes are universal, present in each individual in our species, across cultures and time. They are embedded in our unconsciousness—that is, we are unaware of them mostly. When our archetypes break through into our consciousness, they are individualized so that we each have our own versions of the various archetypes. My version of the Healer and Goddess archetypes is Turquoise Woman. Archetypes come to us in our dreams, most commonly when the barrier between our conscious and unconscious is most permeable and left-brain dominance is relinquished. They can also come in visions and can be called forth into our consciousness in meditation, visualization exercises, and shamanic journeys such as I took to meet with Turquois Woman.

In general, shamanic traditions of indigenous peoples delineate three spiritual worlds: The Lower World, the Upper World, and the Middle World. I have explored all three in my shamanic altered states of consciousness. The Lower World is primal and earthy and where I have usually gone to meet and consult with my archetypes (except for when I have turned to my Teacher archetype/spirit guide). It is this world that is closely tied to MacLean's reptilian and paleomammalian brains (see Appendix 2 for more detailed information on this). It is by far the most interesting, to me, and is where I have spent much of my journey time. It is here that I find my Power Place, an archetypal symbol in itself. It is from here that I draw my real power.

The Middle World is the spiritual aspect of this. The Upper World is pretty boring to me and takes on much of the imagery of Christianity's heaven. However, it is in the Upper World that I first journeyed to meet my Teacher; it is the place of our higher cortical functions.

These three worlds can roughly be thought of as corresponding to Jung's personal unconscious, collective unconscious, and ego, respectively; or to Freud's Id, Super Ego, and Ego. In this regard, shamanic journeys to the spirit worlds are actually journeys into our three personality states. Our normal state is in the Ego state. My shamanic journey to consult with Turquoise Woman given her close ties to the basic processes of nature and reproduction and caring, was a journey to the Lower World.

As I thought about all of this some more, I glanced up once again to the far-off Chisos Mountains, with my hypothetical guru sitting up there looking down on me. I decided that he represented my Teacher archetype in the Upper World. And I decided to call him Charles. Not sure why the name, Charles, popped into my mind. I just accepted it; it sounded right somehow.

Jung reasoned that archetypes help us define, understand, and deal with our world, and, for the most part, are ingrained into our unconscious processes. They are problem solvers, important to our primitive ancestors and even for us today. But what do we know about their underlying neurobiology and genes? If they are inherited as part of our species' DNA, do we have archetypal genes? Where are archetypes located in our brain?

Jung posited that the archetypes primarily operated at the subconscious level. What we call *consciousness* actually only involves an estimated 5% of our brains.[22] The other 95% of our brains are down there operating at our unconscious levels. Consciousness, i.e., that of which we are aware, is built on a huge array of underlying unconscious neural circuitries and processes. As Sam Harris (*Free Will*, 2012) adroitly argues, virtually all our decisions are made at the unconscious levels in the lower parts of our brains, before they ever get up to our consciousness.

To make a long story short, it turns out that archetypes are symbols that help us understand things, in particular, those things that are ineffable or very complex and difficult to grasp. They act as metaphors for our unconscious emotions and complex problems, to make them easier to comprehend and solve. These emotions and challenges are easier to understand because archetypes are innate. That is, they are hardwired into our brains or quickly learned, as they are primarily part of our species' heritage, or secondarily, related to our own personal history. The archetypes are closely tied to our *emotional neural circuitry*. They come to us as dynamic, three-dimensional, stand-alone mental constructions, with emotional content. They are not just abstract symbols and are, consequently, experienced as external. They are experienced in altered (non-ordinary) states of consciousness, such as dreaming, meditation, trances, etc., when the brain can access its deeper, more universal, unconscious layers. Situations that push us out of our comfort zones can elicit them. (For more on the neurobiology of archetypes, see Appendix 1.)

As my first day drew to a close, I breathed a sigh of relief as the sun started setting over my shoulder and behind the mountains in the west. The heat would finally abate, I thought. It would cool down considerably with the setting sun. Right?

No, wrong! As dusk settled in the desert around me and the wind abated, I suddenly was attacked by a horde of mosquitoes. First a solitary mosquito, then several, then many. It was like someone had rung the dinner bell and said, "Come and get it! Hot blood! Yummy!" I frantically scrambled to remove the sheet hanging above me and wrap it around me to keep the mosquitoes from biting me—nasty little bloodsuckers! So, there I sat in the gathering darkness—sweating, wrapped in my sheet. I had been bitten by a couple of them and the bites had started itching, which set off the chigger bites on my legs to itching. I was one pile of misery as I once again dug through my backpack for the cortisone cream and started applying it. It was a long, hot, sweaty night with the buzz of mosquitos around me the full night. I looked out into the dark wondering what other nasty critters were out there just waiting to sneak up on me. From *The Wizard of Oz*, Dorothy's chant of "Lions and tigers and bears, oh my!" came to me as I looked out into the vast desert wasteland around me. Mountain lions, coyotes, and bears, more like it in my case. But then, let's not forget about the scorpions, snakes, and spiders, either. Friendly beasts, all. They love to cuddle.

At one point, I decided that a little light might help lower my anxiety. Reaching into a side pocket of my backpack, I pulled out my old candle lantern, my companion on many camping trips, and my bag of candles that fit it. To my chagrin, the candles had all melted together in the day's heat! Crap! Taking out my pocketknife, I cut one of the candles loose and trimmed down the extra wax that had melted onto it from the other candles. Placing it into the candle lantern, I fished out a lighter and lit it. A nice reassuring flame rewarded me. I placed the glass chimney over the lantern to keep the breeze from blowing out the flame and set the candle lantern on Lajitas' rock, sighing with relief at its mellow, yellow glow. My relief only lasted a few seconds. When I looked back over to the lantern, I realized it was swarming with a dense cloud of mosquitoes and that the bright candle in the dark desert night was like a beacon, probably calling all the mosquitoes from miles around. With a deep sigh, I put the flame out, and sat there looking out over the dark desert landscape.

My anxiety was still pretty high, but my eyes were adapting to the dark and I found I could actually see pretty well now as the moon had started to rise. At that point I noticed that in the far distance I could see a light, probably on a ranch or house. No telling how many miles away it was, but definitely a long way. The full moon, however, was plenty of light for just sitting there, and that was what I did. I can tell you, if you have never sat out in nature, in the dark, by yourself, with wild animals and nasty creatures all around you, you haven't lived. This was only the second time I had done so, and I figured that I had made it through that first time in the desert of New Mexico, I would probably make it through this time as well. After all, Strong Eagle had said he hadn't lost anyone yet, right? It was a long, long night.

The last thing I remembered thinking about was my hypothetical guru, Charles, up there high on the highest peak of the Chisos Mountains to my east. How our relative positions, him high up and me way down here, were similar to *adaptive landscapes*, which I had learned from studying evolutionary biology were about Darwinian fitness. How, in an analogous way, our relative positions represented his greater *spiritual fitness*. And how, in my spiritual growth, I was trying to climb up a higher spiritual mountain by increasing my spiritual fitness. Sometime in the wee hours of the morning, I fell into a fitful, sweat-filled sleep.

4

WARRIOR AND OUR EVOLUTIONARY HISTORY

DAY 2 EARLY MORNING

Medicine Wheel direction: West

Archetype: Warrior (Cougar)

Credo: Stepping up and being present

Key words: courage, appropriate use of power, leadership, and walk-your-talk

"Courage is being scared to death and saddling up anyway." — *John Wayne*

I AWOKE AFTER A MISERABLE NIGHT OF SWEAT, MOSQUITOS, AND VERY little sleep, but—I had survived! I was alive! No lions, tigers, or bears! Well, no mountain lions, coyotes, or bears! I had heard that bears had become a problem in the park area as populations had moved into the protected area of the park from the mountains of Mexico. But those were up in the Chisos Mountains mainly, not down here on the desert floor where we were. Out here with all the nasty cacti, etc., like landmines on the ground, I figured the large predators were not a significant issue. The mosquitos, however, were another matter altogether, as were the rattlesnakes and scorpions.

In the early morning darkness, I had come awake from a dream about my hypothetical guru, Charles:

> I had flown up to his cave near the mountaintop on my eagle archetype, Wind Eagle, sliding off his back when we landed. Before me was the opening to a cave that was lighted within. Wind Eagle had shrunk back to his normal size and was perched upon my shoulder, his usual place. I walked with him through the cave's door. There sitting on a meditation cushion in a lotus position, was Charles. He reminded me of a wizard with his long white beard, similar to Gandalf the Wizard in the Lord of the Rings trilogy movies. He was dressed in a Gandalf-like long white robe and was reading a copy of Richard Dawkins' book *The Selfish Gene*. I cleared my throat to let him know I was there. Without looking up, he raised a finger, indicating for me to wait and then pointing to a sitting cushion in front of him. I sat, assuming a half-lotus sitting position, per my usual.
>
> As I looked around his cave, the first thing I noticed was his large selection of books—books were everywhere. Beside him on his sitting cushion was a copy of E.O. Wilson's newest book, *The Social Conquest of Earth*, and Daniel C. Dennett's *Breaking the Spell: Religion as a Natural Phenomenon*. Distributed around the cave in piles and on bookshelves were collections of books on a wide range of topics, including evolution, molecular biology, mathematics, psychology, theology, Native American spirituality, the Eastern religions of Buddhism and Hinduism, Christianity, and Islam. Quite an extensive library. I thought how I had many

of the same books in my study back home. On a large, ancient, massive, dark wood desk was a reading lamp, what looked like manuscripts, pens, pencils, and a Hugo Reinhold's Philosophizing Monkey statue, the latter being a great ape, studying a human skull, pondering it, and sitting on a stack of books. On two of the books, I could read the titles on their bindings, one reading *Evolution*, and the other, *Darwin*. I smiled.

Meanwhile, Wind Eagle had flown off my shoulder to a large perch that was over against one wall of the cave at its side. He seemed to be right at home. At the side of the perch was a wire-walled canister, about a foot in diameter. He was gazing over into it. Suddenly, he reached down with his powerful beak and came up with a squirming mouse. As I watched, he crushed it in his beak, and swallowed it whole.

I heard a noise and turned my head back around to Charles, who had closed his Dawkins book and was looking at me. Before I could say anything, he raised a finger and said: "Evolution is the Way, the Truth, and the Light."

With that, I found myself emerging from my dream and back at my quest site. In the morning's dim dawn and, thankfully, cooler air, I peeked out from my covering sheet. The mosquitos were gone. Amazing! I would later figure out that it was because of the strong desert wind. As the wind came up while the sun rose, heating the desert floor, the mosquitos disappeared. They had gone to hide and find safety from the wind, I assumed. Throwing my protective sheet off, I stood up, hearing a complaining rumble-grumble from my insides, saying, "Feed me, feed me." It had now been over 36 hours since I had last eaten. I got up and drank some water. My "breakfast," I thought. First checking my boots for any unwanted guests, I pulled them on and went and did my morning bodily needs stuff, outside my circle, urinating over the near arroyo's side in front of God and all his glory.

After returning and sitting a few minutes enjoying the cool morning desert air, sans mosquitos, I decided that I wanted to go ahead and get my morning check-in walk out of the way before it got too hot. The walk was to let Strong Eagle and Grandfather Chasing Thunder know that I was okay—well, still alive and kicking anyway—before the high heat of the day. Each morning of our time alone out in the desert, each of us questees was to pick out a spot, somewhere away from where we were doing our quest, to leave something that let them know that we were okay. We were to leave something out of the ordinary each morning that looked out of place, that would be a signal to them.

Strong Eagle and Grandfather Chasing Thunder did not know where each of us were, only the general direction that we had each headed out. They had no idea where we would pick in that vast desert to leave our signal. I could not imagine them wandering around looking for a spot where we had left a signal of some sort. How would they know it was from one of us and not just a fluke of the desert? For additional "safety" we each had a whistle to use in case of an emergency. I hoped both of them had hearing better than mine. I mean, this desert was so HUGE!

As I went out looking for some place that was noticeable and unique that Strong Eagle or Grandfather could easily spot, I saw some small, pretty stones and picked them up. I would use these to mark my spot and signal that I was OK. A little later, I came across a unique piece of mesquite bush root and picked it up too. Finally, I came to a smooth spot that was clear of cacti, plants, and rocks. Looking around to check my orientation, I could just make out my Turtle Rock quest site, or its direction anyway, and thought I could see the top of the base camp's big tent in the distance. I gathered more stones from around the site and constructed a medicine circle. In the middle of my circle, I placed the small stones I had picked up. Looking around, I came across a long lechuguilla stem and placed it in the center, adding some more, larger rocks to hold it upright, kind of flag marker. I hoped the wind wouldn't blow it down later. That would have to do, I decided, and headed back to my quest site.

Coming back from my check-in walk, I sat on one of the small boulders around me and enjoyed what was left of the morning's coolness. A small fruit fly landed on my hand. At first, I thought it was a mosquito but took a closer look. Nope, it was a fruit fly, sure enough. Holy Shit! That meant there had to be water around here somewhere, at least a small trickle of a stream. I tried to examine it closer without disturbing it. It had a dark abdomen and what looked like two dark hairs—the sex combs they are called—on its rear legs. It was a male, and probably a member of the *Drosophila pseudoobscura* species, which occurred in this region. I had done a lot of research with this species for my doctorate and had collected not too far from here in the Davis Mountains for part of my research. The research had been about genetic variation and natural selection. "Ah ha," I said to it. "Well, hello there, little friend. Long time, no see." At that, he flew off.

Reflecting back on my guru dream, I had decided that today, the second day of my quest, my focus was on Warrior and evolution. For me the evolutionary process was a lot about being a warrior—and my archetype, Cougar—per Darwin's natural selection and "red tooth and claw" perspective. That said, for me evolution also had a lot to do with spirituality and spiritual growth.

There are two broad aspects of evolution: evolutionary *history* and the evolutionary *process*. Both help us to better understand and lend insight into our spirituality and spiritual growth. They also help us to understand the biological basis of religion in general. *Evolutionary history* is about the story of how various species or groups evolved. The evolution of land animals from fish, the evolution of humans from a common apelike ancestor, the evolution of horses, mammals, birds, reptiles, etc. are all evolutionary stories: who evolved from whom and what. *Evolutionary process* is about the underlying genetic mechanisms involved in evolutionary change, which basically boils down to changes in gene frequency in populations: how the DNA itself evolves and the underlying genetic processes. Archetypes are part of our species' evolutionary history.

Cougar, a.k.a. mountain lion, is my personal archetype for the West on my medicine wheel. Cougar is a fierce hunter, the top of the food chain, before humans. When I think of cougar, I think of both Tennyson and Darwin, and their references to the "red tooth and claw" imagery. Tennyson was talking about the brutality of nature in general; Darwin, about natural selection in particular.[23] In cougar and my first meeting, it was my red blood that was on his claws.

Cougar and I first "met" in a training in advanced hypnotherapy in what is known as an altered state of consciousness through a Holistic Breathwork exercise pioneered by Stanislav Grof.[24] When I tried this breathwork, I found myself "awakened" laying head to head with Cougar on the ground; we were looking into each other's eyes, both of us dying, our blood running together. The co-mingling of our blood symbolizing that we were blood brothers. I was an American Indian, Apache, I think. He had disemboweled me with his powerful claws. I had buried my knife to its hilt in his neck. I was not afraid. We both knew this was not the last of our meetings.

You can see why "red tooth and claw" comes to mind when I think about him. He stands for me as the brutality of natural selection as well as nature herself sometimes. Of the forces that cause evolutionary change, natural selection is the Big Dog, Top Horse, Alpha, at the top of the pecking order, etc., in the evolutionary process.

Lajitas was back, I noticed, looking up at me. I said good morning to him and asked, "Come to check on me?" He said nothing, per usual, and scampered off. I continued my thoughts.

Cougar is also my *Power Animal* in shamanic terms, that is, my guardian spirit, from which I draw courage and remember my power— and not to give it away. He is a fearless, powerful, lone hunter. Very powerful hunting medicine. As Warrior, I placed him in the West on my medicine wheel. He reminds me to step up and be present, to have courage even when I am afraid, to walk my talk.

ANIMAL SYMBOLS

Animals have probably been used as symbols for most of *Homo sapiens* existence, and maybe the *Homo* genus in general, given the ancient animal cave paintings of Lascaux in France that date back 17,000 years, and even older ones in Serra da Capivara in Brazil that date back 23,000-25,000 years. Our brains are geared to quickly organize our experiences into animal symbols, probably a testimony to our long evolutionary history and intimate association with them, not the least of which was being both their prey and predators. Our lives depended on them. The evolutionary origin and importance of animals as archetypal symbols goes back to the shared origin and neurophysiology between humans and animals. It was critical for other animals to recognize predators, for example. I work with horses in equine-assisted psychotherapy. Horses recognize humans as predators. Predators are marked by front-facing eyes, whereas non-predators, or prey, by side-facing eyes. Horses have to be taught that we will not harm them.

Our brains seem to innately learn quickly to understand other animals and humans. Darwin, the real father of evolutionary psychology, published in 1872 his famous studies on emotions of mammals, comparing the anatomy and the muscles used in different emotional states for humans, dogs, cats, horses, ruminants, and monkeys. *The Expression of the Emotions in Man and Animals* was his third major book on evolution, following his *Origin of Species* (1859) and *Descent of Man* (1871). He concluded that we and the other mammals use the same muscles for the same emotions.[25] That is why other mammals can read our body language, and we can read theirs so well. They also read our pheromone body signals, e.g., the fear odors we emit. As a zoologist with a lot of experience with a wide range of vertebrates in general, but especially fish; as a mental health therapist who uses horses and dogs to assist in therapy; and being familiar with our small farm and its chickens, goats, and horses; I can certainly attest to that co-communication ability. Even chickens, dumb as domesticated breeds are, can read a lot from our body language. When I would go out to harvest one for dinner, they would run from me. Otherwise, they gather round me wanting food—hopefully leftovers from the kitchen. Chickens are great recycling systems in this regard.

We now know that the underlying neural mechanism we share with other animals is based on specialized neurons called, *mirror neurons*.[26] Mirror neurons fire when we act, and when someone else acts. They enable us to interpret the actions, behaviors, and emotions of others. They also enable us to learn by imitation. This is a very important ability for a highly social species such as *H. sapiens*. Mirror neurons were first identified in rhesus monkeys. They are also found in other primates and animals that have been studied, including horses, dogs and cats, rats, and mice. It is a small jump to comprehend that animals and humans can understand each other and thus their role as archetypal symbols.

Animal symbols come to us in our dreams, often representing unconscious aspects of the dreamer's personality or potential personality. This applies mainly to wild animals, as opposed to domesticated animals.[27] Their *wildness* is an important part of their symbolism. The large cats, lions, tigers, cougars, etc., are associated with our instinctive power. In the past they have stood for transformative forces in medieval alchemy, wild desire, and attacking (ancient Persia). In Christian mythology, Christ was both lion and lamb. Buddha's symbol was the lion.

Animal symbols will often shift from one form to another, and shamanic journeys (altered states of consciousness) can include the shifting to and from various animal forms, a process known as *shapeshifting*. Shapeshifting is about transformation. In my own alternate-state journeys I have shifted from my self-symbol/image, to my cougar, from cougar to a horse, and to my Eagle, all to view things through their eyes.

Our evolutionary history also helps us to understand why we continually have conflicts between our selfish desires and our altruistic "should." The "shoulds" are taught, for example, by the world's great religions and spiritual teachers. For example, the Golden Rule: do unto others as you would have them do unto you; or, love your neighbor as yourself. It is as if we, as a species and as individuals, have a dark side and a light side. Guess what, we do! We have both selfish and unselfish DNA as part of our evolutionary heritage.

5

OUR SELFISH AND UNSELFISH DNA AND CULTURAL EVOLUTION

DAY 2 MID-MORNING

I THOUGHT BACK TO MY CHECK-IN WALK EARLIER THIS MORNING. I HAD come across a large harvester ant bed and stopped to watch it for a few minutes. Over toward one edge, well camouflaged by its desert-mottled skin, sat a "horny toad," as we called them when I was a kid growing up in West Texas. I used to capture them and keep them as pets. They are very docile, relatively slow-moving lizards, armored with spines that protrude from their backs. Plus, they spit "blood" as a defense mechanism, as well as puff up their flat bodies to make them bigger and more difficult for a predator to eat, like a puff fish does. The "blood" they spit actually squirts from two openings on their nose and contains toxins from the venom of the harvester ants they consume as their primary diet. More correctly known as horned lizards, and here in the Chihuahuan Desert, the Texas Horned Lizard to be specific, they are members of the *Phrynosoma* genus.

Harvester ants are a large species' group of ants that harvest seeds and whatnots, and store the seeds, etc., in their nests' communal granaries.

This species' group is comprised of several species that range in color from reddish to black. The invasion of the dreaded fire ants greatly diminished the harvester ant populations, which in turn diminished the horned lizard populations. When I was a kid, harvester ants had been plentiful, as had horned lizards. Now both are rare.

Harvester ants, as well as fire ants, are what is known as *eusocial* species, as are virtually all ant, bee, most wasp, and termite species.[28] As a one-time honeybee keeper on our farm in South Carolina, I had a lot of hands-on experience with eusocial insects, including a variety of ant species (fire ants, red ants, carpenter ants, etc.), and wasps and bees. We humans are also a eusocial species.

Eusocial species build nests, combine multiple generations, and are characterized by altruistic behaviors as part of their division of labor. For the social insects, there is a queen who lays eggs, workers who do the work in the colony, young of various ages, soldiers that guard and defend, and a few token males that act as sperm donors. For example, male honeybees, called drones, are just there as sperm donors, tolerated by their all-female hive-mates. During winter and hard times, the drones are kicked out of the hive, where they quickly die, or are outright killed off by the all-female workers. For humans, there is family and extended family: parents, children, often grandparents.

There are many important differences between the social insects and humans. Among them are size, and numbers; and, very important, each member of the human species is, would be, or has been capable of participating in reproduction. Whereas in the social insects, only the queen is capable of reproducing. Their hives can be thought of as super individuals and all the queen's offspring as phenotypic variants of her genome. If the individuals develop from an unfertilized egg, they will be genetic females like herself. If they are from a fertilized egg, they develop into males. The social insects, like bees and ants, exhibit *phenotypic plasticity*, meaning the same *genes* can take a variety of different body forms. In the case of honeybees, for example, individuals with the same genes can be workers or queens, depending on what diet they are fed.

One of the important characteristics of eusocial species is their *altruism*, defined as self-sacrifice. In evolutionary biology, altruism means lowering our own *Darwinian fitness* as an individual, which means sacrificing or lowering our own survival and/or reproduction potential. Darwinian fitness is a measure of reproductive success. The firefighter who goes into a burning house to save someone or even a pet, is potentially going to get injured or maybe even killed. The police officer, the first responder, soldiers in war, etc., are all acting altruistically, endangering their lives for others. From an evolutionary perspective, are they crazy!? This altruistic behavior and the genes for it, though, are part of our eusocial heritage.

Darwin long ago reasoned that it made sense that, given two groups, one composed of individuals who were willing to sacrifice themselves for their group (read, tribe, village, town, etc.) and a second group that would not self-sacrifice, the self-sacrificing group would have a higher survival value. In other words, natural selection would favor the self-sacrificing group. They would fare better, as a group, than the non-self-sacrificing group. That is, natural selection could take place between different groups, something called *group selection*. Enters the work of E.O. Wilson's extensive studies, along with those of others, which have shown that group selection, as proposed by Darwin, can explain not only our altruism, but also many of the traits of our complex and highly evolved society and culture. The problem is, our DNA is basically selfish. How did we as a species get from our basically selfish DNA to our altruistic, selfless DNA? This selfish vs. selfless DNA question has everything to do with our spiritual growth and deals with a basic, inner conflict of humanity's genomic and cultural evolution. This conflict is why we see such terrible atrocities committed by our human species, such as acts of war, genocide, ethical cleansing, etc.; these also result from our eusocial genes, because of this intergroup selection. This shadow side of humanity is *tribalism* and is part of our tension as a species in our spiritual journeys.

In our quest for spiritual growth, we are continually called upon to balance out the conflicting demands between our primal selfish DNA and our more newly evolved selfless DNA. The irony is that one of the very things that made our species successful and able to show such extremes of altruism, i.e., eusocial group selection, also is the one that created our most evil and destructive tribalism side.

Our evolutionary heritage "tension" as a species has two sources. First, at our most primal level, is the basic selfishness of our genes. Second, as part of our eusocial genes, superimposed as they were later in our species' evolution onto our selfish DNA, is our tribalism. Tribalism is group selection, where different groups (tribes) compete for limited resources. Think here of the stories in the Bible's Old Testament Pentateuch chapters about how conquering armies would commit genocide, killing men, women, and children, Germany's Third Reich persecution of Jews, the ethical cleansings of Africa, racism, the white man's near extermination of indigenous American Indians. Our list, as a species, goes on and on.

(At the time of this writing, I must step out of our story relevant to tribalism and note today's coronavirus new world. Through this pandemic, we can see that polarized tribalism is alive and well such as, for example, the groups of people wanting to re-open the country in spite of the scientific and medical warnings otherwise, and their vocal persecution and threatened violence against those who, trying to respect the science, say it's too early and too dangerous. So too, we see the destructive flames of tribalism being fanned by some politicians for political gain, spreading divisiveness, violence, in-group versus out-group conflict.)

As stated earlier, from the genes' DNA's standpoint, the individual is just a gene's way of reproducing itself. At our core then are the individual selected *selfish* genes. Wrapped around that core or added to that selfish

DNA are our eusocial *selfless* traits. As Richard Dawkins so eloquently argued in his book *The Selfish Gene*, natural selection primarily acts at the level of the individual. It is in our very DNA to be selfish, to look out for number one, which includes our family because they carry our genes too. It all comes down to basic survival and reproduction.

But along comes eusociality, a remarkable combination of traits of cooperation, that results in *selfless* traits, such as altruism—and it changes the ballgame. When the benefits of the selfless behaviors increased the group members' collective fitness sufficiently to override individual selected selfish traits, selfless genes increased in the population and species.[29]

However, for humanity, there is yet another layer atop of our selfish and selfless DNA. After all, we can see the early beginnings of altruism and selfless behavior in other eusocial species and many mammals in general. On top of humanity's basic DNA's evolution is *cultural evolution*.

GENES VS. MEMES

Our civilization is the result of the *coevolution* of culture and genes, which is to say that culture and genes co-evolved. They were interdependent. However, cultural evolution is vastly faster than biological evolution. Speaking of today's world, E. O. Wilson (2012) eloquently wrote, "We have created a Star Wars civilization, with Stone Age emotions, medieval institutions, and god-like technology."

Biological evolution is ponderously slow compared to cultural evolution. Just as the biological evolutionary process is based on changes in the DNA or genes (Chapter 6), cultural evolution is based on changes in *meme* frequencies. Memes are a unit of cultural transmission or imitation, comparable to genes, except at the cultural level, and are ideas.[30] Both genes and memes are replicators: they replicate themselves. And both are transmitting information: genes transmit organic information; memes transmit inorganic information. Living systems, and life in general, evolved because of differential survival of replicating entities, that is DNA: individuals, human or otherwise, are reproducing/replicating systems and some of these survive and reproduce betters than other individuals. This is to what Darwin's "survival of the fittest" really refers. Likewise, cultures evolved due to the survival of different competing ideas, that is memes, compared to biological evolution and the survival of differential competing genes.

Referencing the fable of the race between the tortoise and the hare, genes are the tortoises and memes are the hares. And just like genes, humans, their institutions, and cultures, are the memes' way memes reproduce themselves. Our various religions are an example of memes, as was Darwin's theory on the origin of species by natural selection also a meme itself.

Religion in general can be understood as a natural phenomenon, shaped and sculpted by cultural selection acting at the level of the memes.[31] Most of our spiritual journeys are taken against the background or within one of the world's great religions. Religions are actually collections of complex *co-adapted* memes, which is to say memes (ideas) that work well together to increase their collective fitness.

The day's heat was rolling down on me like a locomotive, and I was lying, tied, to its tracks. Where was Dudley Do-Right when you needed him?[32] It must be noonish, I thought, as I sat sweating under my tarp. I had put the sheet back up as a secondary sunshade again. I was so thankful for the desert's fairly consistent blasts of wind. Not as constant as the first day, but still considerable, and I was relieved to have them. I carefully wetted my bandana and hung it over my head to help cool me down some. I wanted to go easy on the water as I had another full day to go after today, and I had to get through another cooking afternoon with me as the entree. Earlier in the morning, Lajitas had paid me a couple of visits, never staying long, and I couldn't engage him with a chat. He must have a full schedule today.

I looked toward the high desert mountains of the Chisos, and once again thought of my guru, Charles, sitting up there looking down on me. Then thought back to the visit of my little fruit fly friend earlier this morning and the evolutionary process' aspect of spirituality, which also had to do with mountains and gurus.

6

SPIRITUALITY AND THE EVOLUTIONARY PROCESS

DAY 2 AFTERNOON

Figure 6.1. Me on my low spiritual mountaintop looking at my Guru, Charles, way up there on his higher mountain top, across the wide desert valley between us.

THE AFTERNOON'S HEAT ROILED ON, MAKING SURE I WASN'T JUST HALF cooked, but well done. Gazing from under my tarp up toward the Chisos Mountains, I envisioned once again Charles sitting up there on his high mountaintop. Thinking, among other things that it was probably 10-15 degrees cooler up there compared to the desert floor here.

Lajitas hopped back up on his rock at that point, and I explained to him, talking out loud at this point and pointing to the high mountain peaks in the distance, "So, Lajitas, Charles is sitting up there, looking down on me. Not in a judgmental way, but as a teacher watches a student solving a problem. The teacher waits patiently, knowing that he must let the student figure it out for himself for the student to really learn the lesson. So, it is with our spiritual journey. A spiritual teacher is a guide, nothing more. They can point the way, but the student must find it and walk it himself. The teacher can't do it for him.

"I am reminded of a saying from Zen, one of those little zingers they love to use: 'If you meet the Buddha on the road, kill him!' Kind of harsh, no? What it means, though, is that a teacher is only a finger pointing at the moon, he/she is not the moon. Substitute 'Truth' in here for moon, Lajitas. The teacher can only point you toward the truth, he/she can't take you there. You have to find it for yourself. You have to find your own truth." With that, I pointed to Charles' mountaintop up there in the distance. "My spiritual journey is about getting to that, or to a higher spiritual mountaintop." Lajitas didn't speak, just looked at me in the knowing manner of lizards. I wondered if Lajitas was not himself a Zen master. At that, he darted away, and I was alone again. Turning my eyes back to Charles up there, I thought about how our two relative peaks are similar to evolutionary *adaptive landscapes*. His higher peak representing how he had higher spiritual fitness, akin to Darwinian fitness, than I did, indicating he was much farther along in his spiritual journey than I.

Graphically, our two juxtapositions could be represented like this:

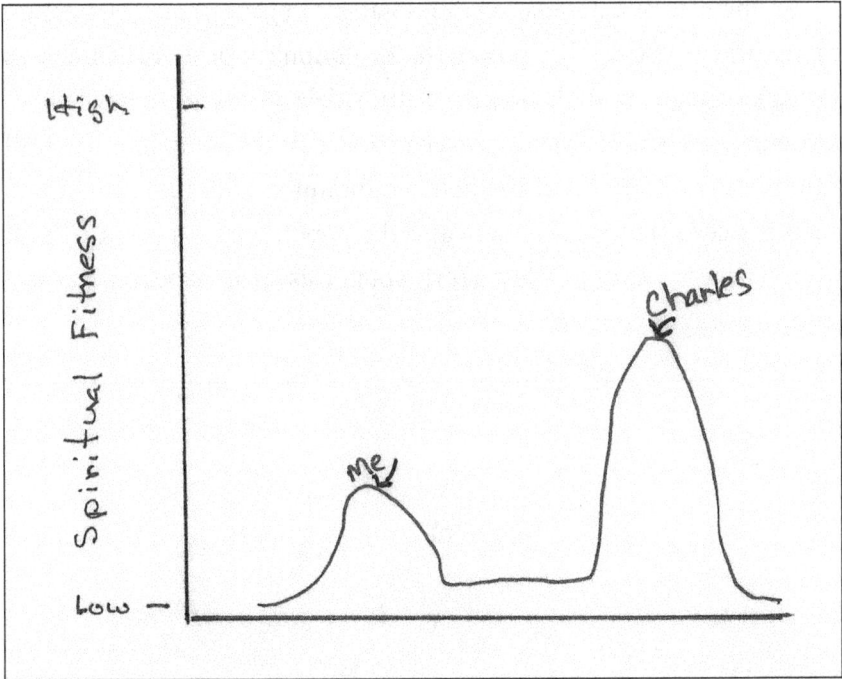

Figure 6.2. An adaptive landscape of Charles and I sitting on our spiritual mountaintops.

My goal was to get up there where Charles was, in terms of my own spiritual fitness. I wanted to be on a higher spiritual plane or mountaintop. Meaning, I wanted to have higher spiritual fitness. What did I mean by spiritual fitness anyways? How would I know it if I had it?

How would I get up there to that place of higher spiritual fitness? I mean, there was a deep, wide valley between us that I would first have to get across. That valley was symbolic and important, I intuited, but I wasn't sure at the moment what it represented. Then, once across the valley, there was a long climb up that mountainside to get to the top. All of this, the two mountains we occupied and that valley, was similar to a population *trying* to reach a higher level of fitness on a Darwinian adaptive landscape. I felt that the answers to my questions would add clarity to my spiritual journey.

In the case of a population, it is changes in *gene frequencies* driven by natural selection that power the evolutionary process. Known as Fisher's Fundamental Theorem of Natural Selection, selection will drive a population's gene frequencies to change so that the population's overall fitness increases and is at the new mountaintop and, then, will act to keep the gene frequencies there and the population at a point of high overall fitness. Let us talk just a little about this term "gene frequencies" using a *gene pool model*:

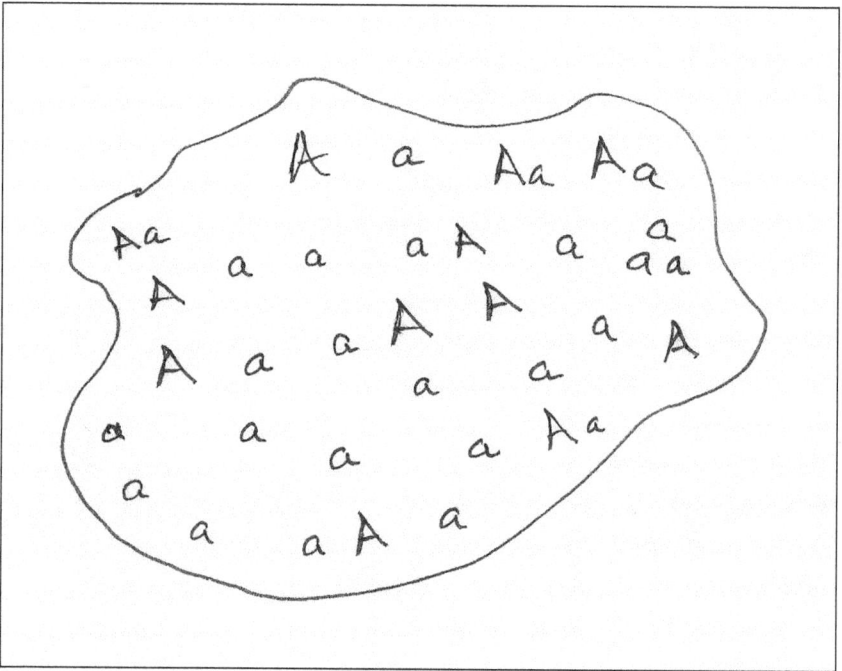

Figure 6.3. A gene pool of a population with two alternative forms of a gene (alleles),[33] A and a. See text for explanation.

Think of a population as a collection of genes (alleles) rather than individuals. We can represent these genes in a pool or pond, just sort of floating around as shown in the above figure. Let us say we have 100 total alleles in the pool with 35 of them the *A* allele and 65 of them the *a* allele. Then the gene/allele frequencies are p = 35/100 = 0.35 for the *A* allele, and q = 65/100 for the *a* allele. The evolutionary process is defined as changes in gene frequencies in a population.

In our hypothetical population above, let us say that the *A* allele was at a selective disadvantage in their current environmental situation compared to *a*. Selection, the primary force that drives evolutionary change, would act to decrease the frequency of the *A* allele over time, thereby increasing the frequency of the *a* allele in the population's gene pool. With this way of understanding, we can now go back to Charles sitting up there on his high mountaintop.

At that point, my hunger got my attention, my stomach growling out that it wanted food again. I took a few sips of water and told it to be quiet. Grumble, rumble, it answered. The heat was really on up there now, approaching its merciless peak for the afternoon, I hoped. Two days in this heat, without food, and in my solitude, I was struggling to keep my thoughts gathered, much less in logical order. Like trying to herd cats, or kids with ADHD,[34] my thoughts would just sort of wander off on their own, easily distracted. I would have to go and gather them back up, get them reordered. My thinking was growing fuzzier and fuzzier. This did not bode well for tomorrow, my third day out here. With or without my attempts to corral them, my thoughts turned to a real-life example about gene pools.

I thought back to my little fruit fly friend that had landed on my hand this morning and the evolutionary genetic study I had been involved in as a graduate student out here years ago.[35] We were in the nearby Davis Mountains collecting fruit flies. My major advisor and I had driven all the way from the University of Georgia, stopping to spend the night with my parents who were still living in Odessa, Texas at that time. On our way out of town the next morning, we had stopped and bought a huge number of bananas and several packages of yeast. My advisor had explained this was the bait we would use to catch the fruit flies. I thought, wait! these guys live out in the arid Southwest, no bananas grow anywhere in the Southwest. He informed me that it was the yeast we would put with the bananas that they were attracted to; they fed on the yeast, not the bananas. Out in the parking lot, we had spent quite some time peeling the bananas, placing them in plastic buckets he had brought, pouring a packet of yeast over each bucket's bananas, then smashing them up. Little did I appreciate at the time that I would be spending the next two weeks riding around in his station wagon with buckets of fermenting bananas that continued to get riper and riper! Luckily, he had lids for the buckets, but by the end of the week, the lids didn't seem to be helping much. It was summer in the Southwest. We drove a lot with the windows down and the AC on full blast. Our first stop was the Davis Mountains.

We were studying the genetic changes in natural populations of this little species of fruit fly: that is, changes in their gene pool. Our part of the study involved surveying populations of *Drosophila pseudoobscura* across the southern part of the southwest U.S., starting with the Davis Mountains. Other members of our research team were covering other parts of the species' range, from California northward up the West coast to Canada. My advisor and I were responsible for Texas, New Mexico, and Arizona. Others were sampling Utah and Nevada populations. The genetic survey marked the 30th year of monitoring evolutionary changes in this fruit fly. The resulting publication would be the 42nd in Theodosius Dobzhansky's series in *Genetics of Natural Populations*. These studies revealed the ongoing complexity of the evolutionary process in natural populations. Collaborating with us on the study was Jeff Powell, Dobzhansky's last student and himself now a professor at Yale University. I was just a lowly graduate student. It was an exciting time for me to be working with such greats. Dobzhansky himself was considered one of the founding fathers of evolutionary genetics, and his many notable students, including my doctoral advisor, had pioneered much of our understanding about genetic changes in natural populations.

What we found in that study was that genetic changes continued. Of course, we suspected that, as we knew that evolution does not stop. But we were documenting these changes in this species across its entire range and over many generations. As the environment shifts and changes, the genetic system of all species continues to change, to adapt. We were documenting and studying those changes.

I was reminded of the Buddhist teachings on *impermanence*: all forms are impermanent. Another way of understanding that teaching is that everything evolves, that is, everything changes; everything is in process. Change/impermanence is in the very fabric of the universe.

In this part of my doctoral studies, we were following the primary genetic changes in the fruit fly's gene pool relative to frequencies of third chromosomal gene arrangements. I was specifically monitoring and establishing a base line for a specific gene on the third chromosome, the *Amylase* gene, abbreviated, *Amy*. Amylase is an enzyme that breaks down starch. It is ubiquitous in virtually every vertebrate species. I had even observed amylase in sharks and the living fossil fish, the coelacanth. *Drosophila* has four chromosomes; humans have 46, plus two sex chromosomes, the X and Y, for a total of 48 chromosomes.

Chromosomes are threadlike structures of nucleic acids (DNA) and proteins that are found in the cell's nucleus. Genes "live" on the chromosomes. That is, the chromosomes consist of large collections of genes. Think of the chromosomes as streets and the genes as houses on those streets. We can think of each cell as like a town. In *Drosophila*, the towns/cells only have four streets/chromosomes. In human towns/cells, there are 48 streets. We have about the same number of genes as fruit flies. This means that for humans, their genes/houses are distributed among 48 different chromosomes. In Drosophila, those same number of genes are distributed between just four chromosomes.

Genes are complicated. For example, genes are more like islands in an ocean. The ocean water in this metaphor is called *spacer DNA*. We have enough DNA for hundreds of thousands of genes, but as we now know from the Human Genome Project, all that DNA only contains some 30,000 or so genes. Most of our DNA is this spacer DNA. Plus, the genes themselves are not a single piece of DNA. Going back to our house analogy, the genes are more like modular homes where all the rooms sit in different spots, linked together with long hall-like intron DNA. These introns, as they are called, have to be edited out for the gene's product to be functional.

In humans and most critters, the chromosomes are teeny tiny. I mean, really small. However, one of the wonderful things about *Drosophila* is their giant *polytene* chromosomes, located in their salivary glands in their larval stages. These giant chromosomes are easily visible under only modest magnification in a microscope. Polytene means that their chromosomes consist of thousands of copies of each chromosome laid side-by-side in their salivary glands. You can easily distinguish the four different chromosomes from each other in these fruit flies in these salivary gland chromosomes—and the chromosomes have different *gene arrangements*. These are what we were studying, these gene arrangement pools, meaning the frequencies of the various gene arrangements in the populations.

D. pseudoobscura is really nice for evolutionary studies because it has *gene arrangements* on only one of its four chromosomes, its third, compared to *D. melanogaster*, the standard workhorse of *Drosophila* genetics that has gene arrangements on all four of its chromosomes. Plus, *D. pseudoobscura* was a lot more fun to collect—out in the mountains of the Southwest. Although, *D. melanogaster* likes breweries. They love the yeast that grows in the fermentation process. That has an upside too in terms of collecting them. So, let's put it this way, I liked collecting

D. pseudoobscura because it lives mainly in the Southwest's mountain regions, and I could bring my own beer, thank you.

These chromosomal gene arrangements of the fruit fly tie up large blocks of genes. I mean, there are a lot of houses on each street, but for the fruit fly, there are only four streets in their little towns/cells. By "gene arrangements," we are talking about how the genes are arranged on the chromosomes—where the genes/houses are located. In one gene arrangement, for example, a particular gene might be located at one end of the chromosome. In another gene arrangement, the same gene might be located somewhere near the middle of the chromosome, and so forth. What these gene arrangements do is to enable the fruit fly populations to rapidly adapt to environmental changes. The gene arrangements also help the populations to maintain genetic variation. Genetic variation is the raw material of the evolutionary process: no genetic variation, no evolution. The more genetic variation, the faster populations can respond to environmental changes. Genetic variation generates diversity and diversity is good.

For those of you that garden, think of how many of today's garden plants are hybrids: they consist of crosses between two different strains. This generates a lot of genetic variation! The hybrids are more resistant to diseases and pests, faster growing, higher yielding, etc. Mules are another example: very sturdy, strong, high endurance, healthy. Mules are hybrids between horses and donkeys.

Early experiments with *Drosophila* showed that even genetic variation generated by random mutations was better than no genetic variation.[36] Genetically identical populations that had no genetic variation were compared to the same genetically identical populations that had been irradiated. Irradiation, in this case X-rays, generates random mutations. The irradiated populations reproduced and survived better than the non-irradiated populations.

In general, evolutionary geneticists have found that natural populations, including humans, carry large amounts of genetic variation.

Much more, in fact, than suspected by even Charles Darwin. Without genetic variation, populations or species could not evolve. The more genetic variation, the faster evolution can occur. Natural selection acts on genetic differences between individuals, and these differences have different *fitnesses*.[37]

What I was doing out here on this quest, was creating a sort of spiritual variation, analogous to genetic variation. I was doing something different, a variant to my usual life, so that a type of *spiritual selection* could act on it, pushing me up to a higher mountaintop, hopefully, moving my spiritual fitness to a higher level.

Charles and I have different spiritual fitnesses, his higher, mine lower as shown in Fig. 6.2 What is the relation between fitness and selection? From evolutionary genetics,

$$fitness = reproduction \times survival$$
$$and$$
$$fitness = 1 - selection$$

In evolutionary genetics, selection is the differential reproductive success of different genetic types. Darwinian fitness is therefore the relative probability of reproduction and survival of a *genotype*, meaning the genes that any individual carries.

From the gene's and evolution's standpoint, the individual is just the gene's way of reproducing it, and evolution is focused on the genes. Genes just happen to be packaged as individuals. Populations are the unit of evolution; it is populations that evolve. Individuals are what selection acts upon, more technically, the genes of individuals. So, individuals are the unit of selection; populations, the unit of evolution.

What the equation above tells us is that the lower someone's fitness is, the greater the selection acting on them is. If you have a fitness of 1, that is the highest possible in this model, you have zero selection acting against you. Another important point to note here is that if either your survival or reproduction is near zero, your fitness is near zero because the relationship between reproduction and survival is a product. If either reproduction or survival is near or at zero, the product is zero or near it.

As an example, you could be the meanest, toughest guy on the block, a regular Arnold Schwarzenegger Terminator, or superman, such that your survival is nearly 1.0. However, if you are sterile, that is, your reproduction is 0 or close to it, then from an evolutionary perspective, that means your fitness is zero no matter how tough you are; e.g., 0.99 x 0 = 0. Your genes have no chance of staying in the gene pool. So goes the evolutionary game.

(*Commentary*. Natural selection and the novel Coronavirus, COVID-19, a force of evolution: Although its precise origins in not yet established, the virus appears to be a *trans*-specific (zoonotic) species, meaning it came from a different species, probably bats in this case, and has mutated and adapted to live in humans. The natural selection it is applying on human populations is enormous. At this count, over 100,000 killed and over, probably way over, nearly 2,000,000 infected, which is only a small fraction that have been tested for the virus. This is natural selection as hard it comes. But wait, that's not all. Then we will be able to add to that all the idiots that are ignoring safety guidelines and themselves become infected. Not to worry though, they are willing to "share the love" (a.k.a. COVID-19), becoming carriers and spreading it further through the human population, even to those trying to observe the safety measures. As I like to say, Natural Selection is alive and doing well!)

To get back to spiritual adaptive landscapes with Charles sitting way up there on his high spiritual mountaintop and me down here on my lower one, the relative differences between us is that Charles would have a fitness of 1, let's say, and I would have a relative fitness to his of, say, 0.5, as an example. Here is a problem with my quest to get up higher to Charles' level. How do I get up there from here? How do I evolve spiritually?

In Darwinian evolution, it is populations that evolve. In spiritual evolution, it is the individual that evolves. In Darwinian evolution, it is gene frequencies that change. In spiritual evolution, it is the *regulation* of the genes' expression that changes. That is because spiritual evolution is a learning process. Learning takes place first in the regulation of underlying genes that then enables *neurogenesis* to take place.

Think of a gene as like a water faucet as an analogy. Let the gene itself be the faucet and the gene's product (protein) be the water. The faucet can be turned all the way off, all the way on, or anywhere in between. Not only that, it is on a timer: it has to be turned on at the right time and for the right length of time. But wait, there is actually a whole battery of genes for which this has to happen to get neurogenesis (brain growth), and these have to be coordinated much like an orchestra playing a symphony. These symphonies are all going on up there in our brains. Then there are other symphonies (groups of genes) carrying on all the body's other functions at the same time. Pretty amazing. Once the right proteins are available, neurogenesis can take place. In the case of learning, neurogenesis involves growth in neural connections, called *synapses*, between the neurons.

In spiritual evolution, changes occur in the individual, not the population, and above the level of the genes. These changes are at the level of regulating the genes' expression that leads to *neurogenesis*. So now we need to talk about these briefly before continuing our journey up the spiritual mountain. Appendix 2 has a discussion in greater detail. Here I will just give a broad-stroke picture.

First, spiritual growth is a learning process. As a learning process, it requires brain growth, called *neurogenesis*, in the form of connections between brain cells (neurons). Learning is a neurological process in which more interconnections are made (and/or strengthened) between the brain cells and/or these interconnections are strengthened. Before these events can occur however, the right genes have to be turned on at the right time and the right amounts, as in our water faucet analogy.

If in Darwinian evolution, fitness is defined as differential reproduction and survival, and selection, the primary driver of the evolutionary process, is differential reproductive success, what drives the spiritual process? My answer is *suffering*. It is suffering that drives our quest for higher spirituality. In terms of our adaptive landscape model, it is suffering that motivates us to seek higher spiritual fitness. It is suffering that drives us up toward a higher mountaintop.

Spiritual fitness then is defined as a product of inner peace and personal growth, and suffering as our dissatisfaction with life as measured by our inner peace and degree of personal growth. (See explanation below.) Or mathematically:

$$\text{Spiritual fitness} = \text{inner peace} \times \text{personal growth,}$$
$$\text{and}$$
$$\text{Spiritual fitness} = 1 - \text{suffering.}$$

What the equation means is this: cultivating inner peace and working on our personal issues lowers our suffering/dissatisfaction. When suffering is zero, spiritual fitness is at its maximum, = 1.

Suffering is a key concept in Buddhist teachings.[38] Buddha's teachings were about suffering, the causes of suffering, and the ending of suffering. Suffering is really an inexact translation of the Buddhist word, *dakkha,* which is better translated as *dissatisfaction.* It covers the whole range of unhappiness, from hard-core suffering to just not being satisfied with our lives or something in our lives. Even being bored is suffering. What does it mean to be on a spiritual fitness mountaintop? It means suffering is near or at zero: *We are at peace.*

What I was doing out there, other than cooking in the desert's heat, was in large part about stimulating my neurogenesis and learning. I was putting myself into some intense suffering, way out of my comfort zone, to increase my spiritual fitness. We know there are three things that stimulate neurogenesis: exercise, variability, and novel experiences. This adventure certainly fit into the latter two.

How to first get across that broad valley between Charles' mountain and this little hill I was sitting on? In Darwinian evolution, populations face a similar dilemma. It is the secondary forces of evolution that can move a population across such a fitness valley. This is because selection will continually move them back up to the peak they are on. Moving off their peak means lowering the population's overall fitness and selection will act to move them right back up to keep the population's overall fitness at a maximum, even though a higher maximum could be achieved on the higher mountaintop. While natural selection is Top Dog, the secondary forces of evolution play this critical role of getting a population across a fitness valley and onto a higher peak. These secondary forces are mutations, migration of individuals, and random genetic drift, which is about a random sampling error that goes on in small populations. But what about spiritual adaptive peaks and getting across a fitness valley such as between Charles and me? This is where intense experiences, like vision quests and Zen sesshins, come into play. Often life itself will throw us out into the "desert" through losses, sickness, and the many other vicissitudes that can create havoc and discord in our lives. These can also lead to new insights and understandings. These are the spiritual valleys of our lives.

Spiritual valleys are dark, uncomfortable, often miserable places. Mystics and spiritual seekers have described them for millennia as *dark nights of the soul.*[39] They are "little deaths," that sometimes are not so little, for which vision quests can be metaphors. These dark times are a time of confusion or undefinedness, in which we wander lost in the wilderness. Think of Jesus' forty days in the desert, Buddha's seven years of wandering, of Abraham wandering in the desert. We will find in the next chapter that these are times of new beginnings, of self-reorganization, that first what has to happen is the old has to die. The old self becomes unstable and falls apart. Then from the pieces a new self can be created. Shamanic traditions speak of this process as disassembly/reassembly.

For us as spiritual questees, we must be willing to walk out into those dark valleys if we want to grow. Either we go of our own free will, or most likely at some point in our lives, we will be thrown out there by life itself—often kicking and screaming! An existential search for meaning and direction. We must cross those spiritual valleys to get to higher spiritual mountaintops. These sojourns into darkness are the very times that great spiritual growth can occur.

Once across a spiritual valley, how do we then move up the mountain to its top? There are two tracks, often intermixed: the racehorse strategy and the plow horse strategy. Somewhere in all my readings back in graduate school, I remembered Charles Darwin characterizing his research and how he worked as more of a plow horse than a racehorse. The plow horse strategy involved slow, hard, persistent keeping at it. This rate of spiritual growth can be supplemented and accelerated, however, by intense experiences.

On the faster, racehorse track up the mountain, we turn to the work of psychologist Ernest Rossi and his *novelty-numinosum-neurogenesis* concept.[40] Research has shown that exercise, variation, and novelty all stimulate brain growth (neurogenesis). Exercise refers to being physically active. Variation refers to doing a variety of things, not the same thing over and over. Novelty means new, different experiences that have not been experienced before. Novelty can lead to the experience of the *numinous*[41], or the holy, which stimulates neurogenesis. Just as high emotions can result in rapid neurogenesis, novel experiences, which also have high emotional energy, can stimulate neurogenesis. Numinous experiences are powerful awe-inspiring spiritual experiences and can lead to a major reorganization of the brain. They are like supercharged *Aha* moments of insight and have high emotional energy.

An example of a numinous experience would be a Christian conversion experience.[42] In Zen Buddhism, numinous experiences are referred to either as *satori* or *samadhi*. Satori means a brief glimpse of enlightenment. Samadhi is enlightenment that opens and never ends. I have been at the satori level several times in my life. Charles is an example of someone in the samadhi stage.

At a sesshin several years ago, I was four days into its seven days when I had a satori experience. My back and legs were killing me from all the hours of sitting, when all of a sudden, all the pain and suffering dropped away. I stepped into a clear, expansive mental space of non-thought. It was breathtakingly wonderful. I wasn't disassociating. I was there fully, mindfully in the now, but there was no *I*. Zen teachings say True Self is no self. I was able to experience my no self, my true self. Wow! Then after about 15 minutes, the door closed, and I was back into my discomfort on the sitting cushions.

Related to these types of experiences are what are called *unitive experiences*,[43] where there is a loss of our sense of self. We see the world and everything in it as a oneness. We understand and experience, intuitively, the interconnectedness of the universe that Buddhists teach about. We experience the world and ourselves in a non-dualistic state.

There is a part of our brains in the thymus that functions to distinguish self from non-self, just as our immune system distinguishes self from non-self.[44] Suppression of this component is probably involved in the unitive processes.

The value of intense experiences such as Zen sesshins and American Indian vision quests is that these experiences pull you out of your comfort zone and stimulate neurogenesis. Such experiences get you across those spiritual fitness valleys. In this regard, these intense experiences then are akin to the other forces of Darwinian evolution: mutation, migration, and random genetic drift.

On a slower, plow horse track across our valley and up the mountain, there is just plain continued, daily practice, i.e., practice, practice, practice... and more practice. Takes longer but still gets the job done. Either track relies on first establishing and building synaptic connections, then strengthening those connections. The nerve cell connections become bigger and faster with use. They start out as a deer trail, then with use, build into a wider foot trail, then a dirt-sized country road, then a two-lane highway, and then an Interstate. The old nerve impulses zipping down a super-highway that our practice has cultivated.

There is yet another dimension we need to consider. It is not just a matter of climbing up to a higher spiritual mountaintop, of gaining higher spiritual fitness, but it is also about staying up there once we have gotten there, something called *equanimity*.

Think of someone that is highly spiritually evolved, someone like my guru Charles up there on his higher mountaintop, for example. In my life, I have met several. Openness, calmness, equanimity, wisdom, compassion, groundedness, centeredness, are some of the adjectives I would use to describe these individuals. Imagine what it would be like to meet Jesus or Buddha! Even if their emotions showed, there was always a central core of calmness or equanimity about them.

A mark of a spiritually advanced person, that is, someone with high spiritual fitness, is equanimity, another key concept in Buddhism. Equanimity can be defined as a conscious, calm realization of the impermanence of emotions and events: they are transient and will pass, so don't get caught up in them, don't attach to them. Equanimity is about acceptance that things are as they are in the moment. In this sense, we can use the term in two different ways: as both a state of being and as a measure of persistence. As a state-of-being it fits the Buddhist definition above. Equanimity can also be used as a measure of persistence: it measures how well one is able to stay on one's own peak where suffering is zero or near zero.

For our model here, equanimity refers to this measure of persistence[45]: how well one is able to stay on one's fitness peak despite all the winds of emotion and changes in our lives. Getting knocked off one's peak means that suffering has gone up and spiritual fitness has gone down.

We can break equanimity down into two components also, *resistance* and *resilience*. Resistance is about how hard it is to get knocked off our peak. Resilience is about how quickly we recover our peak, once knocked off. (Similar arguments can be made for the evolutionary model, by the way.) Everyone, even Jesus, gets knocked off their peak at some point. Everyone has a bad day now and then. Being able to recover quickly from that is important, as is how easily we can get knocked off to begin with.

Coming out of my dazed reverie, I realized that night was settling on my second day. My mind-monkeys had by now grown quieter—a blessed relief in and of itself. Their unrelenting chatter in my brain had descended to a low, background, indistinct hum. Sometimes they are pretty quiet in my everyday life. But a lot of the time, especially when I'm under stress, they can get really loud. The first day out here, they had been quite loud: running amuck, screaming at each other, chattering loudly. Tonight, they seemed to be ready to sleep. Thankfully, my grumbling stomach had also grown quiet.

I grabbed and wrapped my sheet around me in preparation for the hordes of mosquitoes that I felt sure would be moving in again for their feeding. Another hot, sweaty night lay ahead. Again, trying to stay awake as much as possible per Strong Eagle's instructions, I watched as the desert's bright full moon began to make its assent over the Chisos Mountains. Despite my efforts, sometime in the night, I dozed off into a fitful sleep, wrapped in the continuous buzz of mosquitos flying around me and landing on my sheet-covered body.

7

BANDIDO AND HIS SIDEKICK, CHAOS

Day 3 Morning

Direction: North
Archetype: Teacher (Charles)
Credo: Be open to outcome
Key word: Wisdom

I HAD AWOKEN, DAZED FROM DREAMS ABOUT BANDIDO AND MY DRAGON, Chaos. Well, at least I think they were dreams. In my precarious state of mental disorder, maybe they were hallucinations. I was not sure I could distinguish between dreams and hallucinations right now. The first dream had been about Bandido himself, the second about Bandido and Chaos.

Bandido and Chaos are part of my *Shadow complex.* Jung defined a complex as part of our personal unconscious that comes from our life experiences. Complexes are organized around a common theme and are core patterns of emotions, memories, perceptions, and wishes. In this case, the theme was about my Shadow. Like the Cisco Kid and Poncho, the Lone Ranger and Tonto, or more contemporary, the Hobbits Frodo and Sam, Bandido and Chaos were a pair.

In the first dream about Bandido, very early in the morning—

I came awake from dozing off and Bandido was sitting across from me, smoking one of his smelly cigars. "Hey, hombre, how you doin'? Que pasa?" he chuckled. He knew I was not doing well. I did not answer him. His dirty sombrero was pulled back on his head, showing a sun-darkened hat line across his suntanned forehead. His shaggy black hair poked out from underneath his hat. He took a big puff on his cigar, blowing the smoke in my direction, trying to irritate me. The mosquitoes buzzing around me were indifferent to the smoke. Too bad.

He sported well-worn leather pants, tannish and sun-bleached to the hue of the desert landscape. Across his chest were two bandolero bullet belts, forming an "x." His gun was an old Winchester rifle. The gun belts were sparsely filled with old bullets, gray with age and tarnished. Underneath the gun belts, he wore an old, ancient leather vest with beadwork. Its better days were long, long gone. The beadwork was intricate and had been detailed at one time. Now, it just hinted at its artistry. Beneath the vest, he wore a faded plaid shirt. He smelled. On his feet were well-worn cowboy boots. He looked at home out here. He was hardened and grizzled. There was a twinkle in his eye, a sarcastic smirk across his face. He was a piece of work.

His snarky question, the smell of his cigar, and his very presence snapped me back from the fear-abyss into which I had almost fallen. He always seemed to show up when my fear or some other negative emotions were trying to run amuck. Metaphorically, it is Chaos that is running amuck. She is out roaring, belching fire, and causing a general uproar. It is his job to fetch her back to her cave and get her back asleep.

In the desert darkness, Bandido sat there puffing on his cigar, watching me, saying nothing. Just sat, stared, and puffed. His cigar glowed each time he puffed. I stared back at him.

Finally, he spoke again in his broken English, "Hey, Cowboy, what we doin' out here anyway? You don't look so happy."

He called me "Cowboy," not sure why. Maybe it went back to our Harley-riding days—an iron horse instead of a real horse. Of course, now I rode real horses. Peeking out from under my sheet, I answered him, "Hello to you too, Bandido. You know why we're out here."

He took another puff from his cigar, pondering. "Oh, yea, that's right," he said, "Something about talkin' to God, no? Getting' a vision? Couldn't we just have done that back in South Carolina? This is a pretty desolate place. You don't look so happy…and you sound pissed." A pause as he took another puff on his cigar. The mosquitoes didn't seem to bother him at all. After a moment he continued, "So, found any answers yet?" I felt a mosquito land on my nose and fanned it away.

Above me, the black velvet sky was full of brilliant stars, the gigantic full moon shined down on us, lighting the vast wildness around us in an eerie pale light. Infinity looked very big out here in the desert. The stars sat like beautiful diamonds of light: reds, blues, purples, and white ones twinkled against a dark infinity. Back in South Carolina there were so many trees, I could only see small patches of stars. Then you throw in the light and air pollution, the stars there were mere shadows compared to this. I was in awe.

Underneath the sheet, I was sweating and uncomfortable. It was either sweat or mosquitoes. I chose the sweat. I answered him, "I'm pissed because I have no answers, man, no vision yet … and this is no fun. I hate the heat, and I hate these damn mosquitoes." I asked Bandido rhetorically, "Where do these mosquitoes come from, anyway? I mean, this is a desert! Mosquitoes got to have water, man."

Taking another puff of his cigar and exhaling, he chuckled and said, "You whine a lot, Cowboy. Been wantin' to do this for years. You been working for months to come out here, knowing it was not gonna be any fun. You're finally here, and all I hear is whine, whine, whine. Patience not one of your strong points."

He was right, I knew, but I was not going to admit it to him. The old warrior seemed unfazed by the heat or mosquitos. He was a tough old bird. My complaining was the passive-aggressive part of me that I would like to leave out here. It came up when I was under stress or feeling like I had little or no control or power. I certainly didn't feel like I had power or control out here, and I was definitely under a lot of stress. Everything out here was beyond my control—well, most of it was. Even if I said, "screw this," and went back to base camp, I would still be stuck in the heat and mosquitoes for the next several days. Wherever I went, they would be there. Relentless. I'd rather be out here by myself than sitting around the base camp anyway. As an evolutionary biologist, I had to hand it to these mosquitoes. They were very successful at the two evolutionary imperatives: survival and reproduction.

Here they were, a water-requiring species, surviving, and obviously reproducing well out here in a desert, a place with very little water. Ironically, I was one of the available water sources. The females had to have a blood meal to lay their eggs. That meant those flying around me were females. The rains the week before had brought them out in great numbers. For months they had laid dormant, waiting as adults, eggs, or pupae for the next rain. It rained, and there was a furious race to reach sexual maturity, breed, get a blood meal, and lay the next generation's eggs, before their water sources dried up. Nonetheless, I was not happy to be "lunch." I slapped at another one that landed on my arm.

Bandido was right, I reflected, still in my dream. I was not very patient. Patience was not one of my virtues. I had been working on that for years. I had actually made a little progress, mostly thanks to my children, now all grown and parents themselves. Children are great teachers of patience. My grandkids are benefiting from the scars of their parents in this regard.

Bandido showed up mainly when I was stressed out—and I was definitely stressed out now. In my earlier years, I denied him, denied his existence, didn't know he even existed. In my naïve, blissful ignorance, I was dismayed and chagrined when he would step out and take over, often feeling shame about one of his outbursts or behaviors. Now, however, we were well acquainted with each other. He was also my alter ego: I really admired his I-don't-give-a-fuck attitude. Unbridled, he was a shoot-first, ask-questions-later type of guy.

Bandido had what I called a Texas-Ranger attitude. He was the one that snapped at my wife when I was in a foul mood. He was the one that wanted to pound some idiot that pulled out in front of me, causing me to have to hit my brakes and slow down to keep from running into him. He was anger and action to my socialized restraint and compassion. He was not socialized, in fact, or not very, except when it came to the ladies. He loved women! He was the lustful side of my primal instincts. He was survival and reproduction at its most base level. He was rude and crude, and he really didn't give a damn. I liked him! He was the Harley-riding part of me, the real cowboy. No, I didn't care for it when he snapped at my wife. That part of him I had to keep an eye on. I reminded him to be gentler, more compassionate. He didn't do "gentler" well. He was also my dragon Chaos' keeper.

Psychologist Carl Jung defined the Shadow as the denied aspects of self.[46] Our Ego or persona is what we display to the outside world and is either in conflict with our Shadow or in denial of it. Shadow is very instinctual—it embodies those instincts for basic survival and reproduction, as well as other wants and needs.

Shadow can also hold those unexpressed, positive sides of ourselves, such as the masculine side of women and the feminine side of men. After all, as males, we have both feminine (our X chromosome) and masculine (our Y chromosome) in our cells. Shadow can hold talents we have not let ourselves develop.

Shadow can be recognized by its strong affects on us. Whenever a shadow issue comes up, we feel a strong, negative emotion. This gut-level, automatic reflex is often projected outside us towards others in the form of criticism or blame. Racism and bigotry are two of its children. Our Shadow can show itself when we are stressed, lonely, anxious, afraid, sad, feeling shame, and so forth. Also, when we are intoxicated. It can come out like a monster: our very own Mr. Hyde to our Dr. Jekyll.

Neurologically, the Shadow's appearance seems to be a function of the overriding of the cortical prefrontal lobe that regulates complex social interactions and executive mental functions. Basic information from our five senses goes first to the emotional centers of our brain in the limbic system, part of the ancient brain that was once part of the olfactory system. Then it goes to the prefrontal lobe and the rest of the brain. High emotions can easily override the rational responses of the frontal and prefrontal lobes.

Others can see our shadow better than we can. Humans do well at recognizing other people's shadow traits, those parts in others that we dislike or criticize, but we are not so good at seeing our own. Shadow lives in the land of denial. We try to keep him/her there, afraid to stand and look squarely in the face at these parts of ourselves.

Everyone has a Shadow. I recalled a discussion with a fellow church member at a retreat. I had introduced the idea of Shadow into our discussion. She started questioning me about it, asking if everyone had a Shadow? I said, yes, but that some are more aware of theirs and try to acknowledge and work with it. She thought a few seconds and announced to the group, well, she didn't have a shadow. Knowing a lot about her shadow from my interactions with her and having had one of her adult children as a mental health client, I smiled and said something to the effect that some of us were luckier than others.

Personal growth and maturity involve integrating our shadow, as well as working through our psychological issues. Often these are the same because they are highly related. That is, issues and Shadow go hand in hand. We have to acknowledge the denied and repressed parts of ourselves and find healthy ways to give them expression. This was a lot of what I did with clients in counseling.

In my second dream, the one from which I had awoken, my guru, Charles, had taken me down into a dark, dank, nether world:

> ...The landscape was eerily surrealistic, distorted, misshapen, grotesque. It was night and dark. A moon sat high in the inky black sky, barely lighting our way. My boot hit a rock and I stumbled, just catching myself before I fell. Charles was with me, explaining as we made our way through the darkness that this was my subconscious, and we were going to my amygdala, the heartland of my most primal instincts, lizard-brain land, the reptilian brain.
>
> In the murky darkness we came upon a dark black body of water. Its waters were festering, coming to a roil. Standing at the water's shoreline was Bandido, looking out at the large sleeping dragon that lay stretched out

into the lake, her head stuck almost completely into a large black cave opening. She was guarding it, I knew. This was my dragon, Chaos, and Bandido was her keeper. She guarded my inner sanctum. She was the fear that guarded the cave where my innermost, unresolved, unconfronted shadow issues lay like treasure chests. The one place I least wanted to go.

Walking up beside Bandido and looking across the water's blackness at Chaos, it felt ominous, dangerous. There was a stench wafting up from the water that filled my nostrils. My stomach retched. I choked back down the urge to vomit and tried to back away from the water but could not. I realized in a flash of scary insight where I was and said to myself, "Oh, no, Chaos!" She was awakening. Her twitching tails churning the dark waters. The more awake she became, the more agitated, the more her tail twitched. Bandido turned to me and said, "Welcome to my world, Cowboy," chuckling and puffing on his ever-present cigar. He was relentless. I could not get away from him. Wherever I went, he was there.

I turned back and looked across the black waters. Suddenly, the night sky lit up with brilliant orange-red fire. From out of the darkness, the mighty dragon's head was illuminated by the fire pouring out of her mouth. I feared being scorched to death. I looked over to Bandido. It was his job to get her back asleep. He was after all, Dragon Keeper!

With that terrifying sight in front of me, I had awoken from my dream.

It was now mid-morning and the heat was moving on up there as time slowly ticked by. I had taken my early morning check-in walk and was pretty impressed when it didn't take me long to locate the spot again. Strong Eagle or Grandfather Chasing Thunder had left a small, colorful rock inside the circle I had built, as a signal to let me know that they had found it. I had found another couple of colorful rocks on my walk out and placed them inside the circle as today's signal back to them. I had to prop back up my long lechuguilla flower stem marker. The wind had blown it down. I added a few more of the larger nearby stones to help hold it up in today's wind.

Today's wind was more intermittent this morning, gusting enough to threaten my tarp only occasionally. I began thinking back to my dream earlier about my dragon, Chaos, waking and the terror I had felt. I had hoped she would go back to asleep. She could be such a nasty creature when she was up and about ranting and raving.

I knew Chaos well. Whenever I was far out of my comfort zone for long enough, she would come roaring awake. Very unpleasant. And she was roaring now! It was my anxiety, really high now, that had awakened her. She was the fear that guarded my Shadow issues. My anxiety out here was resonating with her, which is what awakens her. Okay, I thought, I need to bring my anxiety down.

Experience had taught me to sit tight, try to focus on what I was doing, which in this case was just sitting there, and not get caught up in her drama and my anxiety. Eventually, she would settle down, go back to her cave, and go to sleep. Easier said than done, of course. At intense spiritual retreats she usually came out on the third or fourth day. I had named her Chaos because when she was out and about everything seemed to turn to chaos, as in, disorder. Chaos, though, has a specific meaning in the world of science and refers to the behaviors of very complex systems, which encompasses most of nature.

As I sat under my tarp looking out over the bleak desert landscape before me, a small tornado-like spiral danced its way across the desert floor below, meandering across the valley between Charles and me. Dust devils are what we used to call them when I was growing up out here in West Texas. Soon I was joined by Lajitas on his rock. In silence, we watched as the dust devil moved along picking up sand, tumbleweeds, and desert debris. It had been a very long time since I had seen one. They were rare in South Carolina where I lived now. Too damn many trees!

After a few moments, it dissipated, rejoining the desert wind from whence it had come. I recalled Strong Eagle's statement before we began our quests about the desert being wild. Dust devils, also known as whirlwinds, were for me symbols of the desert's wildness, I decided: the desert's chaos, self-organization, and awesome creativity. I thought about how our life and spiritual journeys are very much like that dust devil, a metaphor, and how chaos theory's self-organization principle and Butterfly Effect could help us understand our spiritual journey and growth. How small, simple events, let alone major events, could trigger catastrophic changes and reorganization, leading to new heights of understanding—to spiritual growth.

Our lives are like the desert winds, blowing every which-way according to forces that are so often beyond our control. When suddenly in the middle of this chaos, things come together and we become an individual whirlwind, winding our way through our lives. As time progresses though our system, the whirlwind, begins to destabilize. Maybe a change in barometric pressure, a new front or pressure system descends upon us. A major event comes into our life: divorce, death of a loved one, loss of health or a job, etc. We become unstable, and what had meaning and importance before evaporates. Suddenly, we find ourselves once again caught up in the bigger desert wind with no form, swept into events surrounding us, but feeling lost and undefined, no longer knowing who we are or where we are going.

From out of our chaos comes our creativity as we self-reorganize our lives and journeys. We scamper across our individual desert floors for a while, picking up debris and this and that, just as the dust devil out there picks up tumbleweeds, sand, leaves, etc. Then things change, we become destabilized, leading often to increased chaos. We go through a phase of disassembly in a shamanic sense, or death and non-being in terms of a vision quest. Then, after a while, somewhere in the universe a butterfly flaps its wings, and we reorganize into something new. Chaos is exemplified by the desert's wildness. From it we can grow both personally and spiritually.

Vision quests, sesshins, and intense retreats all take advantage of the chaos/self-organization of the mind. They have been an important part of my spiritual journey. Their intensity pushes the practitioner to an unstable point, at which time, the "butterfly" flaps its wings and profound enlightenment and insights can occur. "Butterflies" can be a little ping or a big push. So, where is my butterfly? Where is my enlightenment, my insights? I asked myself over and over out there on the desert and its wildness.

At the word "butterfly," Lajitas, who had disappeared for a while, hopped back upon his rock and looked around. "Ah, Lajitas," I said, "Come to find out about chaos and self-organization—or just the butterfly? First, Lajitas, we need to be clear about what I mean by 'chaos,' then we will get to the butterfly. And, no, it is not the kind you can eat. Sorry." There was a disappointed look on his little lizard face. "However, it includes one of your reptilian relatives, my dragon, chaos."

Chaos refers to the behavior of complex systems that are not in thermodynamic equilibrium, which encompasses virtually everything in nature. That dust devil, this little cactus, you, me, this desert, are all complex, non-equilibrium systems from the standpoint of physics.

Chaos theory enables us to predict the overall behaviors of these systems but not the details. It is still cause and effect, but there are so many different variables involved, we can only describe the overall behaviors of the system. Chaos theory is used, for example, in modeling the weather to make predictions. Non-equilibrium just refers to systems, like the weather or our bodies, that have inputs and outputs from and into the system. Plants take in sunlight, carbon dioxide, and water and convert these to sugar. We eat the sugar, and it powers our bodies, etc. (For more details on all this, please see Appendix 2 where I extend the discussion of chaos theory.) I came out to this desert because my system, that is me, had become unstable in that I was groping for answers, direction, and meaning; for inner peace and personal growth.

When a system becomes unstable, it is at a point where just a tiny shove or ping (think of a poke) can push it in a whole new direction. It will reorganize itself into a new self. Suddenly new insights and understanding emerge. This tiny shove or ping is where the butterfly fits in. Just a small perturbation can cause major reorganization of the system, and the perturbation may not be and is often not even related.

The Butterfly Effect is often described as a butterfly in South America that flaps its wings and sets off thunderstorms in Chicago. There is still cause and effect, the relationships are just too complex and too many for us to understand. Maybe God does, but we mortal humans don't. It would take a super, supercomputer to show the cause/effects, even if we could figure out and measure all the variables involved. Spiritual journeys and growth can, and often are, like this. Such effects can push us across the valleys like the one separating Charles and me, much like the secondary forces of evolution, mutation, migration, and random genetic drift can move a population across a fitness valley.

Meanwhile, back at the ranch, so to speak, Chaos' ranting had settled down as my anxiety had peaked and then dissipated. Again, impermanence. Dissipation, hmm, there's another important concept in regard to spiritual growth and fitness.

It is now noonish, as the sun is directly overhead. I head into my last afternoon out here by myself, Lajitas having disappeared again. Tomorrow morning, I close up camp and head back into base camp. God, I am so ready for this all to be over! I dread my ride back, though, with all the cigarette smoke. Sigh.

8

DISSIPATION-DRIVEN ADAPTIVE SPIRITUALITY (A WORKING HYPOTHESIS)

As the afternoon's heat continued its upward climb to hell, I found myself fading in and out of semi-consciousness, a lot of the time not knowing if I was asleep and dreaming or almost awake and just thinking. I was in that in-between place of not quite awake but not asleep either. That place where the channels between right brain and left brain, conscious and subconscious, are permeable.

Somewhere in that time, I once again found myself back in Charles' cave on the mountaintop. Wind Eagle was perched on his roost and watching me as I walked in. Charles was once again sitting on his meditation cushion and motioned for me to sit down across from him on the other meditation cushion as before. He was reading a scientific journal, pencil in hand, marking it as he read. I looked at what he was reading. It appeared to be a research article by Jeremy England, a physicist and biochemist from M.I.T. After a few minutes, he put the journal down, pointing to it and saying, "This is it! This is the key that ties it all together—the spirituality and the science!" We spent quite some time with him explaining to me how England's work on energy dissipation as the driving principle of the universe was the key to tying it all together. How it all fell into place: sort of a "unified field theory" of spirituality. Later, back in my desert oven, drifting in and out of my semiconscious state, I thought about his theory, and what we had discussed. It was a theory of spirituality that went all the way to the foundation of physics itself and its laws of thermodynamics. The theory was not reductionism. It was not trying to reduce spirituality to physics. Rather, it sought to understand at a foundational physics-level why spirituality was important.

A unified field theory is one of the big areas that has eluded physicists for the last decades since Einstein and the advent of quantum physics. This is a theory that interrelates the four types of energy: electromagnetic, gravity, and strong and weak nuclear forces. At the quantum level of the atom, the world is really a weird place.[47] It is a Wizard of Oz land. Behind the curtain of Dorothy's Wizard of Oz, at the subatomic levels, the universe is not what it seems. Why would such a unified field theory be important to me and to spiritual seekers in general? As I lay there in the heat of the afternoon thinking about it, the answer came, "Because it tied the science and spirituality together! The theory gave a deeper understanding about such spiritual concepts as the Native American's medicine wheel, balance and harmony, resonance, energy flow, and karma, tying these spiritual concepts back to the basic underpinnings of the universe. Charles' hypothesis was that England's Dissipation-Driven Adaptation not only underlies the Darwinian evolutionary process, but that it was also foundational for the spiritual evolution process.

Jeremy England's work is about *dissipation-driven adaptation* and the origin of life itself.[48] The essence of England's new physics theory is that life exists because "the law of increasing entropy drives matter to acquire life-like physical properties." Increasing entropy is called *dissipation.* Another way of stating his theory is that energy dissipation is the driving force of the universe that inevitably led to the creation of life. His research is based on an expansion of the second law of thermodynamics combined with chaos theory's self-organization principle.

Entropy is a measure of the energy available in a system to do *work.* Work here is very specific in physics, but also applies to the *spiritual work* that we do. Work is any force that moves something from place A to place B. As work is done, entropy increases and, unless more energy is put into the system, less and less energy is available to do additional work. Anytime work is done, energy is converted from a higher energy form to a lower energy form, until no more energy is available to do work.

Spiritual growth is about spiritual *work.* That is, it takes work to grow spiritually. In terms of our guru-mountain metaphor, it takes work to get us across the valleys and up the mountainside. It took Charles a lot of spiritual work to get where he was.

Dissipation is the loss of energy that occurs when energy is converted from some form into some other form, which is what happens when work is done. As this process continues, more and more energy is lost and converted to heat. Dissipation then is defined in physics as work plus heat. What drives the universe, England's work proposes, is this dissipation process, where centers of high energy are continuously dissipating their high energy out to the universe—and systems will self-organize to dissipate as much energy as possible, something called *resonance* that I will come back to below.

The First Law of Thermodynamics essentially states that energy of a system cannot be created or destroyed. It is conserved; it merely changes form as work is done and heat is generated. The Second Law, the important one for our discussion, essentially states that entropy increases as work is done

The Laws of Thermodynamics are stated for closed systems for which energy neither comes in nor goes out. These are idealized systems that don't really exist in nature. Living systems are open systems where energy flows in and out. Energy flows into and out of an open system as either work or heat, that is. This is *dissipation*.

Work occurs when energy is transferred from one form to another. Work is a measure of the energy transferred when something is moved from one point to another in the direction of the force that is moving it. This could be moving electrons, mountains, or anything. Heat is wasted energy, essentially. It is energy that is no longer available to do work. Spiritual growth requires work, lots of work.

Keep in mind, energy and matter are the same thing, just in different forms, as shown by Einstein's famous equation, $E=mc^2$.[49] Eventually, if more energy is not put into the system, entropy is maximized, and no energy is left available to do the work. A hot cup of coffee cools down, gases diffuse, batteries run down, boiling water ceases boiling when the heat is turned off, ice cream melts in a warm room. In general, energy disperses or dissipates until it is equally distributed throughout the system and no longer available to do work.

The second law of thermodynamics, referred to as the law of increasing entropy, is also called the *arrow of time*. To understand this, let us turn our attention to particles in a system. Entropy is a measure of how dispersed energy is among the particles in a system, and how diffused those particles are in a space. It is again a measure of randomness. Entropy increases as a simple probability: there are more ways for energy to spread out or disperse than for it to be concentrated.

This is a one-way process, that is, it is *irreversible*, hence the title, "arrow of time." Time only flows one way. As the energy of a system spreads out, it reaches a point where the energy is evenly distributed throughout the system, known as thermodynamic equilibrium. The hot coffee cools if it is left alone to the ambient temperature. The coffee never heats up spontaneously because the probability is overwhelmingly against the room's energy randomly re-concentrating in the cup. Eggs scrambled never unscramble. We grow old; we never grow young. Again, in open systems where energy/matter can be inputted and outputted, our coffee can be kept hot with the constant input of energy, a.k.a. heat. In an open system, entropy can be kept low or at bay through the continual input of energy.

Life does not break the law of entropy. Living systems are open systems and keep entropy low by continually inputting energy to maintain their structure and processes, but thereby increasing the entropy of their surroundings. For example, we humans take in high energy food, along with water, oxygen, etc., convert that energy to proteins, DNA, ATP (energy), bodily structures, and so forth, and give off carbon dioxide, bodily wastes, heat, etc. By the way, these are all forms of work. We give off lower energy in the form of heat, some of which is used to maintain our body temperature. (Death is when our inputs cease, and then, the structures all start breaking down/ decomposing.) Plants take in high-energy sunlight and, through the process of photosynthesis, combine it with carbon dioxide and a little water, converting the energy to sugar, starch, cellulose, and plant structures. This process emits lower level infrared energy and oxygen, thus increasing the entropy in the environment around it. Although life doesn't violate the law of thermodynamics, we were at a loss to explain from a thermodynamics perspective why it might originate in the first place. Hence, the importance of Jeremy England's work.

England's generalized expansion of the second law of thermodynamics applied to systems made up of particles with certain kinds of characteristics and driven by some high-energy source such as electromagnetic waves (think sunlight, lightning), mechanical waves (think waves on the ocean), chemical energy, or so forth, and that could transfer heat into their surrounding environment. This includes all living systems and many non-living ones too. The "certain kinds of characteristics" applies to carbon-based systems. Life on planet Earth is carbon based. England then asked how such systems tended to evolve over time, given that they become increasingly thermodynamically irreversible as they do. (Remember that thermodynamic irreversibility means that entropy increases as these systems offload more and more of their heat into their surroundings.)

His findings showed that the more likely evolutionary outcomes were going to be ones that absorbed and dissipated more energy from their high-energy input. That is, the system restructures itself (evolves) so that it *resonates* better and better with the forces that are driving it. (This is a really important point for our discussion.) The system self-organizes so it can absorb and dissipate the energy better. He points out that the system dissipates more energy when it reorganizes itself so that it resonates with the driving forces. That is, it vibrates in the direction and frequency the driving force is pushing it. Such systems are more likely to evolve in that direction than another direction at any given moment, i.e. toward greater resonance. *Resonance* is a key concept for our purposes here in reference to spiritual evolution, and I will come back to that aspect below.

Resonance can be defined as synchronous vibrations. That is, when two objects (or things) vibrate at the same frequency, they produce the largest possible response/output. If you looked at it graphically, what you would see is that, at their resonant frequencies, there is a large spike in their outputs that falls off rapidly at frequencies on both sides. (For more on Dissipation-Driven Adaptation, see Appendix 2).

For our treatment, think of a mountain and our guru, Charles. At resonant frequency, it is a tall mountain peak. Again, Charles is sitting up there on his mountaintop just resonating away because he is in *harmony and balance* both inside himself and with his environment around him. I will come back to him below.

In living systems, reproduction and survival are the two driving forces of evolution, as we have said. Reproduction, a type of self-replication, is a mechanism by which a system dissipates more and more energy as more and more copies of itself are made and are in turn reproducing themselves. It creates a positive feedback loop where more and more produces more and more. Hence the evolution of life on planet Earth.

Returning this now to our spiritual evolution, could England's work shed light on our spiritual evolution as individuals and why it is important? Charles' answer of course was, yes, else I wouldn't be writing this chapter.

DISSIPATION-DRIVEN ADAPTIVE SPIRITUALITY

Charles' working hypothesis is that higher spiritual fitness leads to higher energy dissipation *as work*, but not just any work, the work that we *want* to do. It leads to higher resonance and harmony, thus magnifying the work output. Because of interconnectedness, a.k.a., Buddhist co-interdependence (interconnectivity), of the universe and with each other, his resonance leads to harmony with others and his environment, which results in further amplification and dissipation through others.

SPIRITUAL FITNESS AND ENERGY DISSIPATION AS WORK

It has been an axiom of what has been known as New Age spirituality that the more we resolve our psychological issues and reach inner peace, the more of our energy we can focus on the things we want to work on and the less of our energy is wasted. This fits in directly with England's research. Less of our energy is used up with dissonance and disharmony, both creating *resistance*. Resistance generates heat and wasted energy, resulting in greater entropy, that is, energy unavailable for doing work.

For example, it takes a lot of energy to deal with our inner conflicts and issues, leaving less available for us to direct toward the things we would rather put it into. Dealing with anxiety, depression, fear, anger, loneliness, worry, etc., is exhausting. They are energy hogs!

Take Freudian defense mechanisms as another example. It takes huge amounts of energy to keep repressed memories repressed. Likewise, denial, distortion, rationalization, etc. From my clinical experiences with patients, I have seen this time and again. I have seen the tremendous wave of relief when they are able to let go of these defenses. Often, my clients have commented about how much more energy they have and how their life is moving ahead. It is unstuck.

I certainly know from my own personal experiences that this is the case. As a recent and very personal example, for the last five years or so, this book has been sitting in limbo. I had been dealing with so much chaos and conflict in my personal life that I had no energy left over to work on the book. Once this conflict and chaos was removed, in divorce, I found my energy and creativity returning. And here we are, writing.

Harmony and resonance are important components here, which will bring us back to the Medicine Wheel.

We want now to look at resonance more closely, as it has importance relevant to spirituality. England's research was on very simple systems, not anything as complex as our minds or any living system such as ecosystems. Again, in physics, the term resonance refers to the amplification that occurs when the frequency of a periodically applied force is at the same frequency of the system to which it is applied—that is, when two systems vibrate at the same frequency. Small periodic forces that are applied at a system's natural frequency produce a high amplitude output of the system. Such amplification or resonant effect occurs in all kinds of systems, mechanical, musical, electromagnetic, nuclear, etc.

For example, take two stringed musical instruments, say a banjo and a piano placed near each other. When one plays a note on the piano, say G4 (G in the fourth octave, or middle G), it will cause the equivalent G4 string on the banjo to vibrate. However, it will also cause the G5, D5, G6,

B6, D7, and G7 strings to vibrate or resonate with it. Actually, it will cause vibrations in all the other integer multiples of the fundamental frequency.

A little relationship worked out by Pythagoras and the basis of our western musical scale, these notes of multiple integers sound pleasing (harmonic) to our human ears. Throw in a half-step note, say D5-flat or sharp, and it sounds disharmonic. I would like to propose that a similar harmonic can be experienced within and between individuals and even between an individual and nature. This is one you can easily test out yourself.

When you meet someone with whom you resonate, you can feel the effect, the heightened energy, the harmony. On the extreme end, "love at first sight" is an example of this phenomenon, but we have all met people with whom we resonate. Likewise, there are places or situations where you have had this resonant effect. I, for example, resonate with the desert mountains; and when writing—that is, when my writing is going well and on some topic in which I am interested. Likewise, for me, there are places in nature that I have felt these really strong resonant effects. The energy vortexes around Sedona, Arizona, are an example. Which brings me back to our guru, Charles.

Charles's working hypothesis was that *the higher your spiritual fitness, the greater your resonance and harmony, the greater your dissipation in terms of the work you want to do.* Greater resonance means amplified output of your efforts or energy. Greater harmony leads to greater resonance effect. If you have ever been in the presence of a powerful spiritual teacher, you can feel these effects.

I can remember in my first sesshin, I was in terrible stress and pain after a couple of days of sitting in silence and motionless for 10+ hours a day, when I had an audience with one of the monastery's teachers. It was a formal interview taking place in a highly ritualized situation. I can remember when I walked into her presence. She was sitting calmly in a lotus position on a mat in front of me. The calm and peace emanating from her was palpable to me: I could feel it, almost taste it, breathe it in. Tears of relief came to my eyes as she gave helpful hints and encouragement. Can you imagine what it would be like meeting Jesus or the Buddha!

KARMA

I am using karma here as simple *cause and effect*. One premise of Buddhism is that everything has a cause(s) and an effect(s). Things do not just happen; they are caused, and they have an effect. Because of our interconnectedness, what we do affects the rest of the universe and others. That effect may be big; it may be small. But remember our butterfly, and now resonance, and chaos theory: even small effects can have big consequences.

This resonant effect occurs as a result of high spiritual fitness. A case in point is my story above about a teacher at my first sesshin. Beyond that though, there is an even greater effect. Positive work that embodies compassion, truth, wisdom, and courage has a harmonic amplification effect on others and the universe. Notice how these four are the essence of the four archetypes talked about in my vision quest. Positive works beget positive work from others, or tends to, and this amplifies the dissipative effects. Likewise, negative work suppresses. When we hurt others, act selfish, or create suffering in others, including other species and the environment, this is negative work. With this, let us now come back to the medicine wheel or sphere.

MEDICINE WHEEL AND ADAPTIVE SPIRITUAL LANDSCAPES

The medicine wheel/sphere symbolizes living our lives in balance and harmony. It is at its center that is where we want to be or stand and live our lives from. That center represents the peak on which our guru sits on his mountaintop, on which we all can sit with varying degrees, that place of inner peace, sufficient personal growth, and equanimity.

INTEGRATING THE MEDICINE WHEEL, ADAPTIVE SPIRITUAL LANDSCAPES, AND DISSIPATION-DRIVEN ADAPTIVE SPIRITUALITY

Process	Component 1	Component 2
Darwinian Evolution	Survival	Reproduction
Adaptive Spiritual Landscapes	Inner Peace	Personal Growth
D-D Adaptive Spirituality	Dissipation	Resonance
Medicine Wheel	Balance	Harmony

Let me bring up at this point, for example, Navaho spiritual beliefs that center on their concept of harmony. Let me humbly apologize to my readers and the great Navaho people. I am basing my comments here on my readings and interest in Native American spirituality, not training in their sacred traditions. With that said, the Navaho tradition has a wonderful holistic philosophy about harmony.[50]

This philosophy encompasses mind, body, spirit, and all our relationships, where health and wellness are linked to their spirituality. This spirituality involves living in close connection to the earth and living in harmony with the environment, nature, and each other. It teaches through stories and legends positive behaviors as well as consequences of failing to observe the natural laws of nature. It focuses on a natural, healthy diet, and practices such as an early morning run to greet the sun each morning.

As the last night of my quest settled down on me, and I wrapped myself in my sheet again to protect myself from the mosquitos, I struggled to stay awake through most of the night. Staying awake was helped by coyotes baying in the distance. An eerie and unsettling sound. At the start, which was late into the night, they were in the distance. As the night advanced, though, they seemed to move closer and closer. Not very reassuring out here by myself and without any weapon for protection. All I could do is toot my emergency whistle if they approached. That kept my tension and adrenalin up through most of that last night.

9

RETURNING HOME

DAY 4 MORNING

Direction: East
Archetype: Visionary/Wind Eagle
Credo: Tell the Truth without blame or judgment

In spring, desert rains bring flowers; in the fall, big moon and coolness; In the summer, dancing dirt devils and scorching heat; in winter chilling winds and clear nights. If useless things do not hang in your mind, any season is a good season for you.

– Zen Poem, modified by Darrell G. Yardley

HAVING MADE IT THROUGH MY LAST NIGHT OUT HERE ALONE—WELL, with the howling coyotes, too—I awoke the next morning soon after dawn. Was I at peace? Hell no. I felt a great deal of anger welling up. Did I feel more grounded, centered? NO! I still did not know how I was going to make a living when I returned home. Absolutely no answers or resolution on that one. Had I gained a much deeper understanding of myself and my spiritual journey? Well, yes. But those insights were rather abstract. I had hoped for concrete answers. Real answers I could use to solve real problems in my life.

Was my brain muddled? Yes. Three and a half days without food, not much water, little sleep, much sweat, a lot of itching, and misery. And the fucking heat! I was so beyond tired of being hot. So tired of this "adventure." Adventure, my ass, I thought, it was more like a stay at Hotel Torture. A mutated version of Roger Williams' song, *King of the Road*, replayed through my mind, but I replaced his lyrics with "No food, no phone, no AC." I wasn't thinking clearly now and knew that only in the years to come, as I processed this experience, would I find ever deepening levels of understanding and insights. For now, I was all mush-mind. I just wanted to get home, back to my family, and the comforts of our family farm.

I spent an hour or so cleaning my camping area, packing, and trying to leave no trace of my being here. Folding up my tarp, sleeping pad, sheet, and sleeping bag and packing them away. The sleeping bag was only used as an additional comfort layer on top of my sleeping pad. I never did crawl inside it. Way too hot. I walked around my vision quest circle, removing the prayer ties I had hung in the four directions. These would be burned in a ceremonial fire that evening. I collapsed my two empty jugs of water by stepping on them, placing them in my backpack. My third and last gallon had only about a third of the water left in it. More than enough to get me through the morning and back to base camp.

After packing up, I sat and looked out over the desert again, up toward Charles' mountaintop. Lajitas popped back up on his rock. "Thanks, Lajitas, for all your listening and checking on me," I said. He bobbed his head up and down twice, turned and was gone. I wondered about Charles' teachings; about all the teachings I had learned out here on this experience. How could I apply them? How could I use them?

As I thought about these, I pulled out the one granola bar I had brought for just this morning. I knew my physiology well enough to know that my glucose level was low, and it would be easy to get disoriented. Brains don't work well if our glucose level gets too low.

Plus, when mine gets low, I get cranky, testy even, which I knew was probably at least part of the reason I was feeling the anger right now. Munching on the granola bar and sipping water, I waited for my light-headedness to dissipate. The last thing I wanted was to get confused and wander around lost out here. Back at base camp would be real food and water.

Would I ever get to Charles' level of spiritual fitness? Not if it had to be this hard. I was past tired of doing these intense experiences. My aging mind-body couldn't handle it like I once could when I was younger.

What were the take-aways from my experiences with Charles, out here? What had I expected to find here, as Bandido had asked, that I could not have found at home? True, it might have taken me longer at home, but, God, it would have been in air conditioning! One of my take-aways I definitely knew was, I was not ever going to do this again! That is enough of this kind of shit for me. No more sweat lodges, no more sesshins, no more vision quests—never again! The chiding voice of Charles sounded in my head, or was it Bandido? "Famous last words, no?" As in, never say never. Never is a very long time.

Getting ready to head out back to base camp, I went around my circle area, pouring the last of my water on the plants and cacti around the site: a little drink here, a little drink there, thanking them for letting me stay here, and saying goodbye to them.

As I started my walk back toward base camp, words and music from America's song "Horse with No Name" popped into my head. I sang, stumbled, mumbled, jumbled, transmuted the words out loud. I knew I was near delirious. The old brain was firing on only half (or less) of its cylinders. I mumbled, sang, "In the desert no one remembers your name." Hell, I was the horse with no name in the desert. I certainly was having trouble remembering my own name. Not to worry, I had my driver's license with me. I slowly trudged down the mountain, across the desert valley, walking eastward.

East is the direction of the Visionary archetype, whose credo is to tell the truth without judgment or blame, and whose key word is truth. Where was my truth, my vision after these four days? East is also the direction of spirit, of which I felt I had little left. To no one in particular and everything in general, I mumbled, "What a waste of time! No burning bushes. No visions. No great insights. Nada. Zip." A few more careful steps and I stopped, modulating my self-commentary, "Well, that wasn't really true. I did gain insights and deeper understandings about the spiritual growth process, interweaving evolution, chaos, and entropy." Again, though, I had wanted concrete answers about my writing and how to make a living. Zippo on these.

In American Indian tradition, the East is the direction of illumination, of spirit, of vision. The Eagle, its medicine animal, sees far in its flight high above the mountains.[51] The East is also symbolic of rebirth in the Native American vision quest. I had been "dead" for three long days and nights in my vision quest circle. This was the morning of my rebirth. What was my vision? What were the truths I found out here? What had I accomplished?

The sun and the heat I had expected. The mosquitos and chiggers had been a surprise. However, I had gotten the chiggers back at Strong Eagle's house back near San Antonio. Whoever heard of hordes of mosquitoes in the desert, for Christ's sake? Back in my growing-up days in Odessa, some 250 miles away, we had had a few mosquitoes, but not the legions I had faced out here. I hadn't brought any insect repellent. It had not occurred to me why I would need it. Besides, Strong Eagle had warned us that its smell would become overpowering as we got into our quest and breathed the clean desert air.

He was right. Yesterday evening, I couldn't stand my own smell any longer. It had been five days without a bath while dripping gallons of sweat. Using some of my precious water, I had given myself a "field" bath. When I put on my deodorant, a supposedly neutral-smelling brand, the odor of just the little bit of perfume in the deodorant nearly made me sick. I turned around and washed off the deodorant. If I couldn't stand even the weak smell of the "odorless" deodorant, I certainly couldn't have handled the strong smell of insect repellent.

After a few steps, I stopped. Then taking a few more steps, I stopped again. Strong Eagle had instructed us that this walk-a-few-steps-then-stop method would confuse the rattlesnakes. I hoped he was right. Before taking the next step, I used my walking stick, a six foot-long, dead dried flower stem from a lechuguilla plant I had picked up, to poke over the rocks in front of me before stepping down. So far, I had not seen any rattlesnakes, but I knew they were about. I was in no mood to deal with one now. I just wanted to get back to base camp and be done with this quest.

Yes, I knew that such experiences stimulated neurological growth and learning—but at such a high price! Was it worth it? Only time would tell. Right now, I could barely think. So, I tried to quit thinking and just walk, and look where I stepped.

I was walking carefully to avoid stepping on plants or critters. At this point, it was not so much my concern for killing or harming something in nature. It was more so that I did not want to injure myself by stepping in the wrong place. My pack and sparse camping gear on my back felt heavy, and I was breathing hard from my exertion. I was light-headed, weak, having trouble concentrating—and getting dizzier with each step. Base camp was only about a half mile ahead.

Granted, as my quest progressed, as I had moved deeper into the fasting, the heat, and the isolation, my head had become clearer and my thoughts sharper. The mind-monkeys' chatter in my brain dropped away. I realized, with even greater clarity, that I already had answers to many of my questions. I had figured these out before coming on this adventure. I felt ripped off. These were the *old* answers. Through this vision quest, I had wanted *new* answers—major, earth-moving insights. What was I doing here, enduring all this, if I did not get new answers?

As I continued my desert walk, up ahead I could just make out the tent top of the base camp in the distance. I paused to adjust my backpack a little. There would be food, water, and other people at the camp. And most important, protection from these damn mosquitos. Being introverted, the "other people" part was not particularly important to me. Getting away from the mosquitos was. Tonight, we would process our quest with Strong Eagle.

As I had walked through that final quarter mile in the desert air that morning, I did not know that in my debriefing that night with Strong Eagle, I would discover another important teaching of this quest for me. It would show me the wonders of chaos theory in action!

At base camp, I was greeted by Strong Eagle and Grandfather Chasing Thunder. I had been the first one to depart for our quest four days ago, and I was the first one back. After an hour or so, the others wandered into camp. We sat on a beautiful Pendleton blanket, ate fruit, drank water and fruit juice, saying little, all stunned and subdued by our experiences. Strong Eagle informed us that he would meet with each of us individually that evening to debrief.

We were to rest and take it easy the rest of the day, but to go easy on the fruit and juice as our systems could not take them in large amounts. Sure enough, a few minutes later, Travis, who had downed a large helping of orange juice and eaten several of the fresh fruits, had an urgent call of nature, and went scrambling for the latrine shovel, disappearing over the small hill Strong Eagle had designated as our latrine area. Quite a few minutes later, he returned, looking pale and obviously not feeling too well. He went through this off and on for the rest of the afternoon, until Strong Eagle gave him some anti-diarrhea medication.

That evening after the sun had set, we were gathered around the campfire. Strong Eagle walked up and asked who wanted to go first? No one spoke. We just sat there looking at each other over the flickering flames. No one was raising their hand or moving. Finally, I said, "I'll go." Strong Eagle and I walked off into the desert night by ourselves.

After we had gone some distance, far enough away that we could not be overheard, we sat down on a pair of boulders and he said, "Tell me about your quest." *"Where to start?"* I wondered. I paused for a few seconds gathering my thoughts and then began recounting my quest. "It was hell," I started. "It was a battle, a test of endurance from the first day until the end." I then began describing the quest, starting with the first day and briefly moving through the next three days of torture. He stopped me and asked, "I noticed you have not said much about the land, your experience of the land?" I gave some lame reply and then admitted that I had difficulty connecting with the land—it hit me: after all my lectures and writing about connecting with the land, I got here and failed. I felt blocked. Something I had wanted to do for years, and I had failed!

He had pointed out repeatedly that there was no way to "fail" a quest. What happened, happened and that was the way it was supposed to be. Before I knew it, I was discussing my finances, my spirit work, my writing. He listened in silence; his head bowed. I ended with saying, "I no longer know what my passion is. I used to know. But it too seems gone."

After a long silence, Strong Eagle spoke, "You know, Darrell, you use the same words to describe your quest, finances and spirit work, writing your book, where you are in your life right now. They are all terms about enduring and confronting, battling."

In that moment, epiphany! The butterfly had flapped her wing! As he continued to talk I realized how enduring, battling, confronting had always been my way of dealing with life—of attacking the things that got in my way. The realization came in an ever widening circle, just as the concentric circles radiate out from a stone thrown into the middle of a still pond, the rings of comprehension moving ever farther from the center. I was nearly breathless with the implications of my realization and his words. *Confronting, enduring, battling.* Whenever I encountered a problem, a challenge, that is what I did—I confronted, battled, endured—until one of us won or I was too tired and exhausted to care. A comment from an old colleague came to me about my charging in. Same thing.

Even back in my karate days, I didn't wait for my opponent to come to me. I went to him or her. Throughout my whole life, I had used this approach. Enough of the time, it had worked, but it was no longer working. This was a dragon I didn't know about. And he was big, huge, awesome—and sneaky. How had he stayed so well hidden? It didn't matter. I saw him now. This was a Shadow Side of my Warrior Archetype.

Strong Eagle continued, saying that up on my mountain that was what I had been doing—battling, enduring, fighting—and Mother Nature sent it back to me seven-fold. She was going to get my attention one way or the other. The harder I would fight, the more she would send it back at me larger, over and over, for three long days and nights. But in my life, I realized, God or the universe had been returning it to me in so many other areas—all seven-fold. I was broken. A great Wind went out of me. She had won. Now what?

Strong Eagle paused and said, "Darrell, whatever you send out will come back to you seven-fold. Instead of fighting, enduring, confronting, why don't you try dancing with it?" I thought of Turquoise Woman's dancing and getting me to dance with her. This is the message she was sending me—about dancing. He continued, "Instead of responding with fear, anger, and frustration, ask them to dance. Ask to dance with your finances." *"How do I dance with my dragon, my demons?"* I thought. Then in a cascade of realization, I began to understand how this applied to other areas of my life.

I thought about dancing and energy flow. When you dance, the energy *flows*. When you confront, the energy is *blocked*. Wow. It was tai-chi versus karate. Tai-chi is about energy flow. You use your opponent's energy flow to turn it away or back toward him. In karate, it is a confrontation. I thought back about Charles' energy flow, dissipation, resonance, and harmony hypotheses. Here, with dancing, opponents become partners. So simple. So profound. I looked at Strong Eagle and said with a smirk, "You know, I would have figured this out— eventually." We both chuckled. *In how many lifetimes?* I wondered. Understanding wavelets continued to spread through my psyche. When the energy flowed, creativity flowed, and there was greater opportunity for solutions.

"What about my passion for my writing?" I asked. When I started this part of my journey, part of it was to write. Now, even my writing seems stymied. After a minute or so of silence and thought, Strong Eagle answered that each day I was to do at least one thing to create beauty. "Give your wife a back rub. Let her know in little ways that she is loved and appreciated. Plant a flower. Weed your garden. Get rid of some clutter. Write a page in your book. Each morning when you wake up," he went on, "wake up thinking about what you are going to do today to create beauty, instead of worrying about all the things you have to get done today." What a wonderful idea, I thought.

Strong Eagle continued, "By creating beauty in one area, you send beauty out into the world, and it will come back to you seven-fold in other areas of your life." "Cool. Non-linearity. Chaos Theory alive and well."

What I had been putting out to the universe was fear, dread, anger, negative emotions, and they were all coming back seven-fold. If I focused instead on creating beauty, then beauty in one form or another would come back to me. What a wonderful way to live!

It occurred to me later, lying in my tent, safe at last from the mosquitoes, and looking up to the star-filled sky through the mosquito netting, what a powerful experience this had been after all. What I thought was a waste, a wreck, and a shamble, Strong Eagle's insights and words had shown me instead a tremendous gift of knowing. Now, it was up to me to put it into action, to use my new understanding and integrate it into my life. Truth without action is just smoke.

THE JOURNEY HOME

The next morning, we began our journey home. We drove most of the day back from Big Bend, then had a group dinner prepared by Strong Eagle's wife at their home. In the late evening Grandfather Chasing Thunder drove me to the airport, a mere 1.5-hours away. We stopped, though, for a few moments at his house en route. The plan was that I was going to get a room near the airport, get a few hours' sleep and clean up, and get up in time to get to the airport and through security for my 6:50 a.m. flight. That was the idea.

By the time we got off the exit ramp for San Antonio Airport, it was 1:30 am. Incredulously there was not a single motel/hotel room in all of San Antonio that was available. There were a number of conventions in town that weekend we were told. (It was now Sunday morning.) We had stopped at eight to ten different motels. No vacancies. To help me out, several of them had called around to other hotels, with the same results, no vacancy.

I was beyond tired—and my smell from days on the desert without a bath could melt concrete. Grandfather and I both sat in his dark pickup trying to figure out what to do. Neither one of our brains were functioning at a very high level. He laughed. I laughed. Oh, brother, what a way to end my Vision Quest. The irony. I thought about Strong Eagle's "dancing" and that I was already being handed an opportunity to "dance."

I was down to $51 in cash. I figured I had enough money to just make it home. It had already occurred to me that I could get to the airport early and sleep in one of the chairs—or stretch out on the floor. I wasn't proud. There would be air conditioning and no mosquitoes, and plenty of water. Compared to where I had been in the desert, this would be heaven. However, when we got there, the airport was closed. So how do you "dance" with a closed airport? Only a few guards stood watch over the mostly darkened building. And, when I glanced inside, the chairs were of hard plastic and very uncomfortable-looking. There was no carpet on the floor, just cold hard linoleum. I talked to one of the guards, explaining my situation. He said, sure I could go on in and wait for the airport to open. No problem.

So here we were in the dark in Grandfather's truck. He said, "Well, at least you're equipped for it?" "What," I asked, "What do you mean, equipped?" You have all your camping gear. You are just camping in the airport. "Of course," I said slapping my palm to my forehead. I had not even thought of that. We unloaded my gear, said goodbyes, and, as he drove off, I carried my stuff into the airport.

I headed directly for the restroom to clean up. When I got there and started running water into the sink, I reached for my knapsack which had my soap, shaving gear, etc. in it, along with my journal and other personal items—and, no knapsack. I had left it in the back seat of Grandfather's pickup, which was now speeding back to his house, some thirty miles away. "Oh great," I mumbled, "Another chance to dance. Will this Quest ever end?" I proceeded to give myself a "field bath" using the airport dispenser soap and paper towels. (If you've never done this, don't.) No deodorant, no toothpaste or toothbrush, but at least with a quick wash, I did feel better, and I'm sure I smelled a little better... like institutional soap. I felt pity for whoever had to sit next to me on the airplane. I changed clothes.

I went back out, pulled my sleeping pad off my backpack and my inflatable pillow and sheet out of it. The sheet reeked from my being wrapped in it. I groaned at the thought of sleeping under it. Settling down, I stretched out in front of the ticket counter and pulled my hat over my eyes to block the ceiling lights. Everything would be alright. I would be back with my family in a few hours.

An hour or so later, I was rudely awakened by loud clanging, scraping, sweeping, mopping, and talking. I peeked an eye out. It was the cleaning crew. I heard them talking about me but closed my eyes and tried to go back to sleep. I said to myself, "Hey people, quiet please, can't you see I'm trying to sleep here?" Over the next few hours, I slept and was awakened intermittently as they went about their tasks. The next thing I knew, the cleaning noises had gone, replaced with people talking. Removing my hat from my eyes, I saw the smiling faces of two airline workers behind the ticket counter. Getting up, I explained to them what I was doing. They smiled and said that they had seen it before. I asked if I could go ahead and check in. They said, "Sure."

Two hours later I was in Dallas, arriving back in South Carolina around noon. It was my youngest daughter's 23 birthday. We were having a celebration at 2:00pm. I had made it! I was back home!

PART TWO

Fifteen Years Later

10

RETURN TO BIG BEND

I HAVE JUST RETURNED FROM WHAT IS PROBABLY MY LAST TRIP TO BIG Bend. A farewell trip to my life growing up in West Texas: visiting my parents' graves, a final meal of chicken-fried steak and French fries at Mary's Cafe in Strawn, Texas, driving by my boyhood town of Odessa, going to dinner at Johnny's BBQ there for the last time, out to Big Bend and back. A trip of farewells.

I had a lot of time to reflect in my four-day drive out there and three-day drive back, two days camping in the backcountry of Big Bend, two days of attending the International Chili Cookoffs in Terlingua. This had been my own mini-vision quest with the two full days and nights camping out on the desert. This time I was accompanied by my two therapy dogs that I now use along with the horses in the counseling work I do.

In an ironic and symbolic twist, I camped on the west side of the Chisos Mountains this time, compared to the eastern side where I had camped on my vision quest 15 years before. Back then, on those four mornings, I watched the sun rise in the east over those mountains. This time, I watched its setting over those same mountains. A metaphor for my life and that trip at this point. East is about visions and new beginnings. West is about closings and endings.

This will be my last trip out to the desert, and I have come to make peace with its wildness, and, perhaps, peace finally with my own inner wildness. Again, another metaphor. Back then on my vision quest, I was at a new beginning, a transition point, a point of bifurcation in my life from a chaos perspective. Now I am in my sunset years. The big difference is that now I am, indeed, more at peace than ever before. Back then, I was in turmoil. For the most part, I have hopefully become more like my guru, Charles, sitting on his mountaintop.

The two therapy dogs that I took with me on this last trip are Morgan and Lacy. Morgan, a.k.a., Old Dog, is a black, ten-year-old Retriever mix. Lacy, white, is a 14-month-old Great Pyrenees. Still a lot of puppy in her. Morgan is also Top Dog between the two of them. Lacy may be younger and outweigh him by some 35 pounds, but there is no doubt who is the Boss Dog.

After we had spent the four days driving out to Big Bend from South Carolina, we were exhausted from all the road hours in the truck. Once you pass the entrance into the Park, it is still about an hour's drive to the ranger station to get a camping permit, then another 20 minutes around to the turnoff to the backcountry and our camping site. Then, an hour and ten-minute four-wheel, high clearance drive from the turn-off. We arrived mid-afternoon and just laid around for a few hours before setting up camp. Morgan liked the back seat of the truck and was sacked out there. Lacy was lying out in the shade of the bear box, a heavy-duty metal box you keep your food and trash in to keep it away from the bears, javelinas (peccaries), etc.

After my rest, I started setting up camp. It was a warm afternoon, but not too hot. After I put a tarp up for shade from the sun and had set out my cooking table and camp cook stove, I pulled out my bottle of single malt scotch and a cigar. Sitting in the afternoon sun, watching the sun preparing to set behind the Chisos Mountains in the West, I reflected on my vision quest trip out here and my return home afterwards.

In the years that followed my return from that quest fifteen long years earlier, my life underwent numerous changes. I never heard again from anyone from the quest, including Strong Eagle. I do not know how the others' quests went. For some reason, we didn't talk much about them, even on our long ride back to Strong Eagle's house. I can remember we were supposed to do a closing sweat lodge ceremony when we got back to his house. Something happened, I think it was raining really hard, and Strong Eagle decided to forgo the ceremony. I, for one, was thankful. The last thing I wanted was more sweating, more heat. Just give me air conditioning and a cold beer! That was my last vision quest and my last sweat lodge.

I did attend one final Zen sesshin after coming back, a couple of years later. I decided afterwards that that was enough! Since then, for a long time now, I have done no more intense retreats. The tremendous power of them is the fact that they stimulate neurogenesis and bring you up against your issues. But then, life has a way of doing that anyway. I never did participate in any of these intense spiritual experiences that I could call "fun." Very beneficial and growth-stimulating, but not fun in any sense of the meaning. They were all just plain hard work. Do I still recommend them to others in their spiritual journeys? Absolutely. They can be powerful, life-changing experiences.

So, here is where I am now after all these years:

SECULAR SPIRITUALITY: A PERSONAL GOD IS AN UNNECESSARY HYPOTHESIS

In all of this I have arrived at a secular definition of spirituality.[52] I now see the personal concept of God as archetypal, and an unnecessary hypothesis. The Big Guy/Gal in the sky was a solution in our primitive past to our species' existential grappling with birth and death, and our feelings of near helplessness against the vast powers of nature, including weather, predators, disease, famine, etc.

As for death, everything dies, even us. This was, and is, a terrifying realization, brought on by our higher level of consciousness—the metaphorical Tree of Knowledge in the metaphorical Garden of Eden. This is a hard, bitter pill to swallow—our own death. To make peace with that is a major goal and accomplishment as we advance toward the ending of our own life. At least, it is my goal at this stage of my life. I want to approach my death with peace-of-mind and equanimity.

I watched in agony my father's struggle three years back. He was terrified and fought his death with every breath. In the end, he was little more than skin and bones, and under great suffering. I spoke to him just minutes before he died on the phone. He could only listen. My parting words to him were that he could let go now. We would take care of our Mother, as much as she would let us anyway. My wife who was there holding the phone to his ear said she could see him relax as I talked. A few minutes later he was gone. I hope not to die like that—with that much fear, suffering and agony.

When I am asked, I say I am a *religious naturalist* and that my spiritual practice is primarily Zen Buddhism. Thrown into this mix is some Christianity, Plains American Indian spirituality, Stoicism, Jungian psychology—and of course, a whole lot of science.

I like to cook, and one of the things I cook well is chili. Good old hot and spicy chili! If you look at my spiritual practice from a chili perspective, Zen Buddhism is the foundational basic meat; while Christianity and the others are the chili powder and various other spices that go into it. (I also do a mean Cajun and regular Tex-Mex.)

Religious naturalism starts from the premise that there is nothing outside of nature; that nature is all there is.[53] That means, nothing supernatural. No transcendent entity outside of nature. No God up in the sky overseeing and running things. No Divine Consciousness or Ground of Being other than Nature herself. No personal God.

More technically, I would call myself a "process naturalist."[54] I see the world in terms of ongoing processes and interrelatedness—a very Zen Buddhist perspective. In Western culture, this is not too far from Whiteheadian Process Philosophy before the God-stuff was added. Each moment is alive and becoming, with things/forms coming into existence and other things/forms perishing. Impermanence and change are the rule. Interconnectedness, Buddhist co-interdependence, is a fundamental part of nature. Nature is relational.

My religious naturalism is not a form of "theology" because there is no *theo* in my "ology." *Natural theology* posits the existence of a God/Creator, and that the laws and processes of nature are how God acts in the world. This God/Creator does not necessarily imply transcendence or anything supernatural. Darwin was a natural theologist.

I might go on to explain to my hypothetical questioner/listener, if she had followed me to this point and was still interested, that I consider the God hypothesis null and void. An unnecessary variable thrown into the equation that really doesn't explain anything. I might further qualify this statement however, by saying that a *personal god* is also an unnecessary hypothesis. By *personal*, I mean a God that is a person, personality, or has "thingness."

To explain this, consider what is called Occam's razor, also known as the law of parsimony, a famous, not so informal rule of problem solving in science. It basically states that the simplest solution is most likely the right one—or at least where you want to start. In the sciences, it means, go with the simpler solution first. If it doesn't explain enough of the variation that you are seeing, then you can start adding additional variables. Now, it is not an ironclad rule; more of a "guideline" (for example, Captain Jack Sparrow's sense of the pirates' rule, in the film *Pirates of the Caribbean*). It is the place you want to start. In this sense, I see the hypothesis of a Personal God out there somewhere directing the universe as wholly unsupportable in the light of science. Natural Laws and processes will do.

Okay, what about a *non-personal* god? In this sense, the whole god concept could act as a metaphor for Nature's laws and processes. Remember, ancient humans had absolutely no concept of natural laws or science. The world was a big hostile place for them. No wonder they would pray to a variety of gods, each in charge of some element of nature, to save them.

The closest I can get to a God in this sense, is more like the *Tao* of Taoism, or the Buddhist Void. Very non-personal. The Tao and Void have no thingness. They are not a thing. They cannot be named or understood. They are ineffable. They can be apprehended, though.

I recall watching Bill Moyer's interviews with the late mythologist, author, Jungian advocate, and Buddhist philosopher, Joseph Campbell on PBS. Campbell was telling Moyer of a meeting he had with a priest. Campbell had stopped into the church to sit a few moments in its quietness. It was a sacred place. A priest who was there began pressing him about a belief in a personal god. Finally, the priest gave up and said something to the effect of, "Well, I guess you just have to have *faith!*" To which Campbell replied something like, "Father, I don't have to have faith. I have *experience.*" This is where I am coming from.

I am lucky enough to have had experiences of the Tao or Void. It was instant experience of the interconnectedness of the universe, bringing an energy into my body that held a peace and serenity that was beyond my understanding, beyond words. One of these types of experiences I had while riding through the South Dakota Badlands on my Harley (I wrote about it in my book *WindWalker*); another was during my last Zen sesshin, mentioned earlier. I have had other, shorter experiences of this underlying reality of the universe while gardening and doing other activities. You don't need faith, if you have experience. *Mindfulness* is the key to having these experiences yourself.

SPIRITUALITY WITHOUT A GOD?

I have defined spirituality in terms of inner peace and personal growth. Can you have spirituality without a God/spirit to worship? I would ask,

"How do you worship gravity, the laws of physics, evolution, entropy? Why would you want to?" So, yes, you can have spirituality without a God. You can be thankful for the good things in your life, without needing something or someone to be thankful to.

To ancient humans, the world could be a terrifying place. (Actually, the world is still a terrifying place at times.) Throughout their cultural history, humans have always prayed to some higher power to allay this terror and help them. They felt powerless quite often and have for millennia looked for answers outside of themselves, devising various kinds of theisms to help them and not feel so powerless. These ranged from pantheism to monotheism. Atheism leaves you with no one to pray to for help or strength. Sometimes, I wrestle with this even today: I miss Jesus and a loving God. There was a comfort there that is gone for me now.

WHERE DOES EVIL ORIGINATE?

I don't believe there is an evil per se. That is, no evil supernatural entity out there is creating evil and chaos. Evil is just accidents and shit that happens. Someone is unfortunately at the wrong place at the wrong time and is hit by a car or drunk driver. God didn't do it. The devil didn't do it. The accident is random; it is not predetermined in the sense that it comes from some supernatural being. Accidents are cause and effect; not fate; not ordained out of nowhere. An earthquake, tornado, hurricane, famine, disease, flood—why do they happen? There is no God, or nasty Satan, up (or down) there doing these. They are natural processes at work, and we just happen to be in the way.

In my four-plus years of theological studies (a year of Old Testament, a year of New Testament, a year of church history, and a year of theology), I recall listening to and reading time and again how Christianity tries to explain evil from a loving, omnipotent God, one of Christianity's big bug-a-boos. What intellectual gymnastics, I thought. What rationalizations! And this was while I even still considered myself a Christian. The problem is, you can't rationalize evil through religion. Evil and a loving, all-powerful supreme being/God are simply not congruent.

If we want to look to where much of the "evil" we see in the world, we can ascribe it to our dark side as both individuals and a society. Another way of saying this is that we as individuals have Shadow sides. At the individual level, our Shadow and selfish genes are always looking or wanting to look out for number 1. At the societal level, we have tribalism. Again, keep in mind that both of these, Shadow and tribalism, have their positive benefits both in the present and in our species' past.

The foundations of our social values and ethical judgments as a species were shaped by natural selection and the evolutionary process. These social values and rules were what worked, and natural selection capitalized on them. As outdated and antiquated as some of those might be, they are part of what made our species successful.

Take the Ten Commandments of Moses. Those codes of behavior were the product of natural selection, not Jehovah. They were shaped by the evolutionary process itself for group-selected altruistic traits. Honed for tens of thousands of years (or more), they were codified as the Ten Commandments in Hebrew history. Stone tablets on a mountain written by God? Just a story as a vehicle for expressing them. They were "written" by natural selection in our genes to help ensure the tribe's (group's) survival. Groups or tribes that followed the "Commandments" were more successful at surviving and reproducing.

DEATH AND DYING

Beliefs in life after death in Buddhism (reincarnation) and Christianity (resurrection) reflected the belief systems of their cultures. (Actually, if you study Christian Biblical history, Jesus's resurrection mythology seems to have been added long after his actual death.)

In my view, the Stoics were more on track: when you die, you die. Das Ende. Finis. Kaput gehen.

Like the stoics, I now believe when I die, I will just cease to be. My body will break down into its recyclable parts. I will be "resurrected" or "reincarnated" but only in the sense of being part of a daffodil or tree or grass for the horses or deer to graze on. In that way, I will return to being one with the universe. In thermodynamic terms, I will be in equilibrium. Entropy for me will be maximized. My thoughts and consciousness will be no more. I no longer believe in anything like a soul.

What about all those near-death experiences or past life experiences that you may have read about?[55] Aren't they real? No, they are not. These can be explained scientifically as archetypal imaginings as the brain shuts down, a psychological defense mechanism, hallucinations, release of endogenous psychotropic substances, and others.[56] They are related to brain physiology and what happens as the brain is dying.

As for past-life experiences, I have had a few of those, as have my counseling clients when under hypnosis or trance. It is interesting to me how those experiences all related to what was going on then and there in my or their life at the time. These seem to be created imaginings of our mind's desire to find solutions and meanings, and more readily explained as projections by our subconscious.

TOWARD A POSITIVE PSYCHOLOGY OF HEALTH AND WELLNESS

Spiritual growth, with its focus on inner peace and personal growth, leads to a positive psychology of health and wellness. In contrast, Western medicine classically focuses on pathology, with little emphasis on emotional health, psychological resiliency, inner peace, or holistic wellness. Wellness is much more than the absence of disease. It is a state of physical, mental, and social well-being. It is much more global and holistic.

Wellness requires supportive relationships, emotional and psychological resilience (equanimity). We are social and tribal organisms. These are in our genes. Social relationships and a sense of belonging are a must. We also need to feel connected to something bigger than ourselves. This latter does not require a supreme being, gods, or angels. Rather it can be our community, humanity, nature, the universe. Or, back to Lakota spirituality, *Mitakuye Oyasin*—all our relations, or, all are related. From an existential perspective, wellness also requires that we feel that our life has meaning and purpose. We need passion to feel alive and that our life is worth living; that our life matters.

Other factors of wellness:

- *A feeling of mastery and self-control.* Wellness requires that we feel more or less in control of our lives. That we are not helpless victims blown by winds outside our control. That we have an internal locus of control over our lives. Yes, there is a lot we can't control, but there is a lot we can.

- *Lowered consumerism; more is not better.* In our Western culture we have been sold a bill of goods, not the goods themselves. Everywhere we turn, buy this or buy that—and you will be happy. *Things* may make you "happy" for a short time. Soon their newness wears off, and you search around for the next thing that will bring you "happiness."

- *Happiness is an emotion.* It is ephemeral like all emotions. What you are striving for is inner peace, which is a *state of being.* Emotions are the underlying psycho-physiological response of our body-mind. Feelings are the conscious mind's awareness of those responses. With inner-peace, emotions come and go without disturbing that inner sense of being. It is hard to remember that, when you are in the throes of anger, sadness, loneliness, etc. This is what equanimity is about:

bringing yourself back to your spiritual mountaintop when your emotions/feelings knock you off—and also being more resistant to being knocked off in the first place. This ability takes practice, as in *spiritual practice.*

- *Mindfulness and wellness go hand in hand.* Mindfulness is the ability to stay fully present in the moment in whatever you are doing, and, at the same time, maintain a global, but unfocused awareness of the world and others around you. It is *not* being lost in a video game, book, or some other activity to the exclusion of what is going on around you.

- *Optimism.* Psychological well-being is healthy. Wellness is about a sense of well-being, which encompasses optimism. Studies have found, for example, that optimistic people are 18% less likely to die of all causes of death compared to pessimistic people.[57] Optimistic people take better care of themselves (lifestyle, exercise, etc.); take action rather than collapse (again, that internal locus of control that my actions will help); and have good social support systems.

What about my archetypes that I talked about back then? Are they still part of my life? Well, yes, but in a different way. They are problem solvers and reminders. They remind me to be open to outcome (Charles), to speak truth without judgement or blame (Wind Eagle), to step up and be present with courage (Cougar), and to pay attention to what has heart and meaning (Turquoise Woman). I seldom go into an altered state of consciousness to communicated with them. They operate for the most part in my neurological background. Reminding me of their credos as issues or challenges pop up that I need to solve. I am aware of them as I go through my day. On rare occasions now, I will enter into an altered state to consult with them when I am stymied or facing a particularly distressing situation. This is done in my morning meditation sitting usually.

Let us end this story with my guru, Charles, on his mountaintop. What might be his parting words to us? Hmmm. Maybe he would say something like, "Be still and know that we are all God; that it is all God. There is no not-God." Or, maybe, "We are the way, the truth, the light. Be at peace." And, "Oh, yeah, watch out for the mosquitos, badgers, bears, rattle snakes, peccaries, and nasty cacti."

EPILOGUE
DESERT MINDFULNESS AND SIMPLICITY

As my last trip to the deserts of my past came to a close, on my drive back home, north out of the Big Bend desert area, I was headed toward Alpine, then to cross over and catch I-20 heading east, saying my farewells as I went. The dogs were peacefully sleeping in the back seat of the truck, my mind was also peacefully at ease. I realized that it was as if I were driving across a vast desert ocean, populated by the occasional desert mountain island. There were virtually no vehicles on the road, only the endless desert plains, my truck, the sleeping dogs, and me. A place of immense solitude, stillness, and simplicity. My mind was wonderfully, mindfully still as I ate up the miles. This was mindfulness, simplicity, stillness, peace at its finest.

In my mind, I saw the occasional lone-standing mountains I passed as metaphors for "thought islands." I could go and visit if I so chose, or not, to think about this or that. The very occasional car or truck would pass from the south. I would think that they were like passing thoughts or emotions—they come, they go, impermanence. I don't get attached to them; they disappear into the desert distance.

On my right, a long freight train passed, headed in the opposite direction. Ah, I said to myself, a longer train of thoughts. But I didn't get caught up in them, and they too disappeared into the desert's vastness. I was incredibly at peace. Glad to be headed home, more than ready to be home, seeking my titanic peace-ness to match the ocean-desert's peace-ness. I knew too that I was headed back to make more changes in my life as I brought this oceanic-desert peace-ness back home; planting it and nurturing it, where simplicity, self-reliance, and mindfulness ruled.

Even though I live near the foothills of the South Carolina mountains, my yard's landscaping is populated with desert flora in some of its high sun areas. I am lucky: in an ironic twist of the universe, Clemson University's South Carolina Botanical Garden has a rich collection of Trans-Pecos desert plants. It has a whole Southwest Desert exhibition area, which interestingly is exceeded only by Texas A&M's collection, with many of the plants from the Big Bend area. I have volunteered my time there in the past and have gotten in return some Big Bend castoff cacti, yucca, and agave species that are happily growing in my yard. Our wet winters are a little rough on them sometimes, and I have to cover them with plastic to get through the coldest of them.

I also have a big garden and grow a lot of my own food—organically. Since I do equine-assisted psychotherapy, I have access to an ample supply of horse manure. Plus, I compost from kitchen waste and make my own compost tea. I preserve much of what I grow by canning, freezing, and drying, especially the chili peppers of which I grow quite a variety. These I cook with all year round.

I have a large, well-equipped shop, which contains a woodworking and general shop area, a mechanical/metal shop, and a garden shed/wash area. I do a lot of my own maintenance, repairs, and fabrication. The credo that I try to live by is reduce, repurpose, reuse, recycle, compost, and simplify.

In all of this, I try to cultivate mindfulness and simplicity. I am still working on Strong Eagle's "dancing" after all the years. Well, I am still working on all of it, to be truthful. Charles, always having to remind me to practice them. As Bandido pointed out, patience is not one of my strong points, and all of these require that I be patient with myself and with whatever I am doing.

As a recent example of the dancing, for decades I have "suffered" with early morning awakenings, getting only five hours of sleep on many nights. Nothing I have done has seemed to help—and I don't do drugs (a.k.a., meds), as they mess up your deep sleep and dream/REM cycles, which are important for mental health, not to mention, letting your archetypes get through to your consciousness. To "dance" around this problem I take naps and when I awake before dawn I simply go ahead and get up, drink a cup of tea and journal, or start working on a book project, or read. Short of it, I don't fight it.

And, yes, my guru/teacher Charles is still in my life. He has to remind me frequently to "picks myself up, dusts myself off, and gets myself back up on my equanimity mountaintop." He reminds me to be mindful in whatever I am doing and to "dance" with the many challenges of my life as they come up.

The irony of this entire journey is that Charles is really me, and I really didn't have to go anywhere to find me. I was there all along. I didn't have to go to the desert and do that vision quest. I didn't really have to do all those intense Zen sesshins, etc. It was me up there on that high mountaintop, just as it was me down below on that lower mountaintop. Granted, it would have taken me longer to get on top of that mountain without them, to figure all this out—or maybe not. Who knows?

All that said, and contrary to prior declarations of "Enough!", I am set to attend another intense Zen sesshin-like experience. This one will focus specifically on all that subconscious stuff that keeps coming up when I do these intense experiences. The stuff that my dragon, Chaos, guards down there in those subconscious parts of my reptilian and old mammalian brain parts. I'll let you know how it goes.

APPENDICES

APPENDIX 1
NEUROBIOLOGY OF ARCHETYPES

MUCH OF THE NEUROBIOLOGY BELOW FOLLOWS FROM ERIK D. Goodwin's *The Neurobiology of the Gods: How Brain Physiology Shapes the Recurrent Imagery of Myth and Dreams* (2012). Here I reiterate and expand on the material presented in chapter 3. Pausing for a costume change: I slip on my professor/academic hat and white research coat. Okay, I'm ready now, clearing my throat.

As Goodwin points out, humans are a symbol-making, metaphorical-thinking species. Far below our language and verbal thinking conscious mind in our outer cerebral cortex, lie our much larger, alive and well, unconscious symbolic and metaphorical processing centers that go on in our lower brain centers. These lower brain centers are the older parts of our brains that MacLean called our reptilian and paleomammalian brains (*The Triune Brain in Evolution: Role in Paleocerebral Functions*. 1990). This is important not only because archetypes are part of these lower brain centers, but also because archetypes, at least our most critical ones, are closely connected to our emotional brain centers, that is, our *emotional neural circuitries*, which are part of the *limbic system*, and which are also housed in these lower brain centers. Understanding a little about how our brains evolved helps us to understand our archetypes and ourselves better. Evolution builds on what it already has; so read on for a little more on MacLean's triune brain.

MacLean divided our brains, in order of their evolution, into the reptilian brain, the paleomammalian brain, and the neomammalian brain, each built on top of and from the other. If you look at a typical fish brain, it is laid out linearly as shown here:

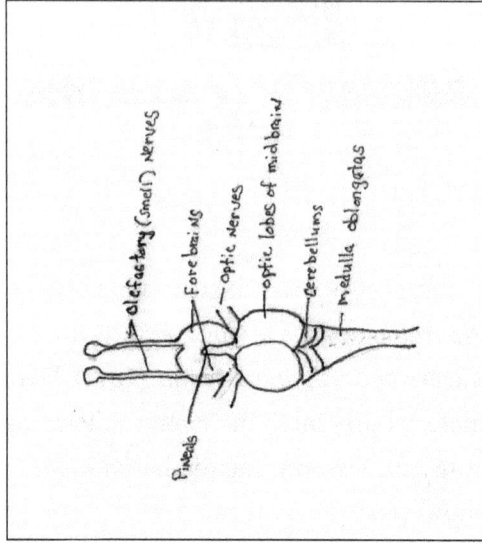

Figure A2.1 The basic fish brain. See text below for explanations.

As shown, the fish brain is laid out linearly starting with the forebrain in front, the mesencephalon behind it, which is made up of the in-between brain and the pineals (small, paired endocrine glands in the brain that secrete melatonin, which regulates sleep and circadian rhythm). Behind the mesencephalon comes the metencephalon, then the spinal cord. Remember, the brain, like our bodies in general, is made up of two halves, the left and right sides. The forebrain will evolve into the cerebral hemispheres, the thalamus and hypothalamus. Behind the forebrain comes the mesencephalon or mid-brain, and behind that, the metencephalon, followed by the cerebellum, medulla oblongata, and spinal cord.

An axiom of developmental biology is that ontogeny recapitulates phylogeny. This is a fancy way of saying development of the embryo replays our evolutionary development. The developing embryo goes through our evolutionary heritage. First is laid down a fish-like brain structure, representing the first early vertebrates, which then proceeds to develop into the highly complex human brain, going through a reptilian brain, a paleomammalian brain, and finally the neomammalian brain. Again, reflecting that evolution, each stage building on what it already has. A course in classic comparative anatomy can be quite interesting.

Going up the old evolutionary ladder and skipping the amphibians, the reptilian brain is only a little advanced from the fish brain, as shown below in Figure A2.2. Reptiles are a little smarter than fish on the old IQ scale, but not all that much. I mean, as an ichthyologist (fish-ologist and someone who used to like to go fishing), I can tell you there are some pretty crafty fish out there. Fishing is like studying religion: the best way to lose your religion (for fishing) is to take a bunch of serious religion courses, the enlightened kind, not the fundamentalist kind. (We're talking Harvard or Yale vs Bob Jones here.) Getting a master's degree and doing research on fish evolutionary genetics is a great way to kill your love of fishing. Sigh.

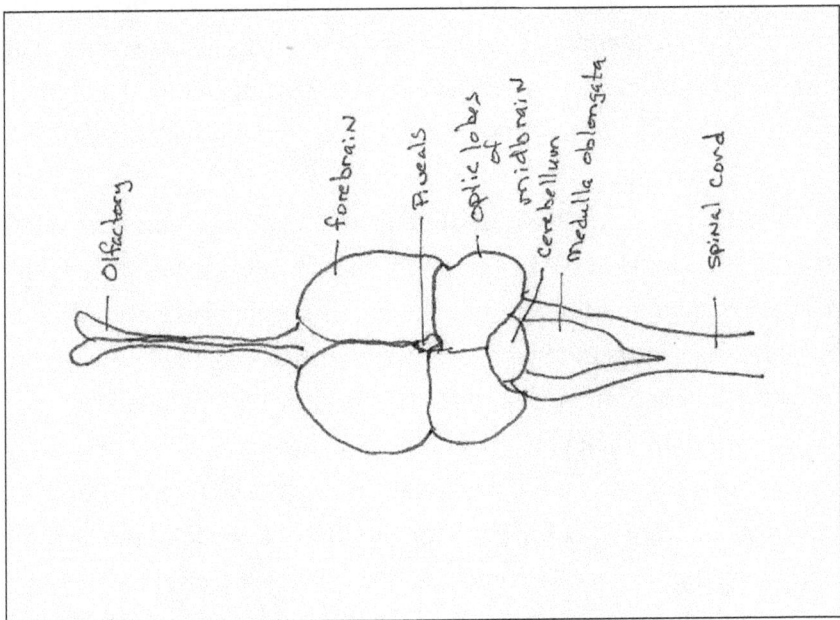

Figure A2.2 The reptilian brain. See text for explanation.

As indicated, in general the typical reptilian brain has the basic structure of the fish brain but with expanded forebrain and cerebellum. The cerebellum controls body movement, suggesting it is a little more complicated, being on land (reptiles) versus living in the water (fish) in terms of movement. Also, reptiles have a lot more complex musculature. Walking takes a lot of different muscles even if you are a lizard, compared to swimming. To get this expanded brainy material packaged, the reptiles had to build a bono fide cranium to house it. A process, of course, started in amphibians. The basic fish brain structure is preserved in all vertebrates.

Moving on up the evolutionary tree to mammalian brains, say rabbit or rat, we have further enlargement of the forebrain, which has now become the cerebral cortices, thalamus and hypothalamus. Folding of the brain has started to cram more brain in the cranium's limited space to accommodate carrying and giving birth to young. Giving birth to live young was a real kicker for mammals: the heads could only be so large and still be able to get down the birth canal. This statement ignores those strange marsupials in Australia that carry their young in a pouch: and especially the duck billed platypus, which lays eggs. Did they miss the bus when the rest of the mammals were evolving? Yes.

At this point, we have arrived at MacLean's paleomammalian brain, which is conserved in all mammals. Among other things, the paleomammalian brain contains the *limbic system*. Variously defined by neuroanatomists in regard to which structures comprise the limbic system, it is more of an association by function, involving some structures of the neomammalian brain as well as the paleomammalian brain.

The limbic system is also known as the *emotional brain*. It processes information from various parts of our body and determines their emotional significance. Its processing is at the subconscious level. By the time that information gets to our consciousness level, the limbic system is already calling on the body to respond. The reptilian and paleomammalian brains are pretty much responsible for our instinctive behaviors and emotions.

The last to evolve and form on top of the reptilian and paleomammalian brains is the new mammalian brain, called *neomammalian*. It contains our consciousness, our higher problem-solving functions, and our logic circuits. It is composed primarily of our greatly expanded cerebral hemispheres, which are further enfolded to increase surface area and brain computing power.

In terms of the limbic system, the reptilian brain contains the basic instincts and primitive survival strategies, such as escaping from predators, i.e., the flight-or-fight response. To paraphrase an old cowboy saying, "Get out of Dodge or fight!" This circuitry is housed in the amygdala. The reptilian brain is conserved across all vertebrates. Reptiles are not very bright, but adequate if you be one. They have a poor sense of humor, and very limited range of emotions. I mean, have you ever seen a happy lizard? Lizard's emotions are probably limited primarily to something barely above approach and avoidance, and fight or flight, though these are behaviors, not emotions. Lizard Love, while allegorical, is probably non-existent. I have had a lizard hiss at me, and I think one bite me too. Is this anger? Only a lizard would know for sure.

The higher emotions are primarily the function of the limbic system evolved in the paleomammalian brain. Mammals in general, Darwin showed early on, have a much broader range of emotions than reptiles and their basic emotional repertoire appears similar to humans, using the same musculature.[58]

As great apes and humans evolved, more and more brain had to be crammed into the cranium. This was done by folding the original linear fish brain back upon itself, and finally, in humans, with their greatly expanded cerebral hemispheres, by folding these into mountains and ridges (Fig A2.3).

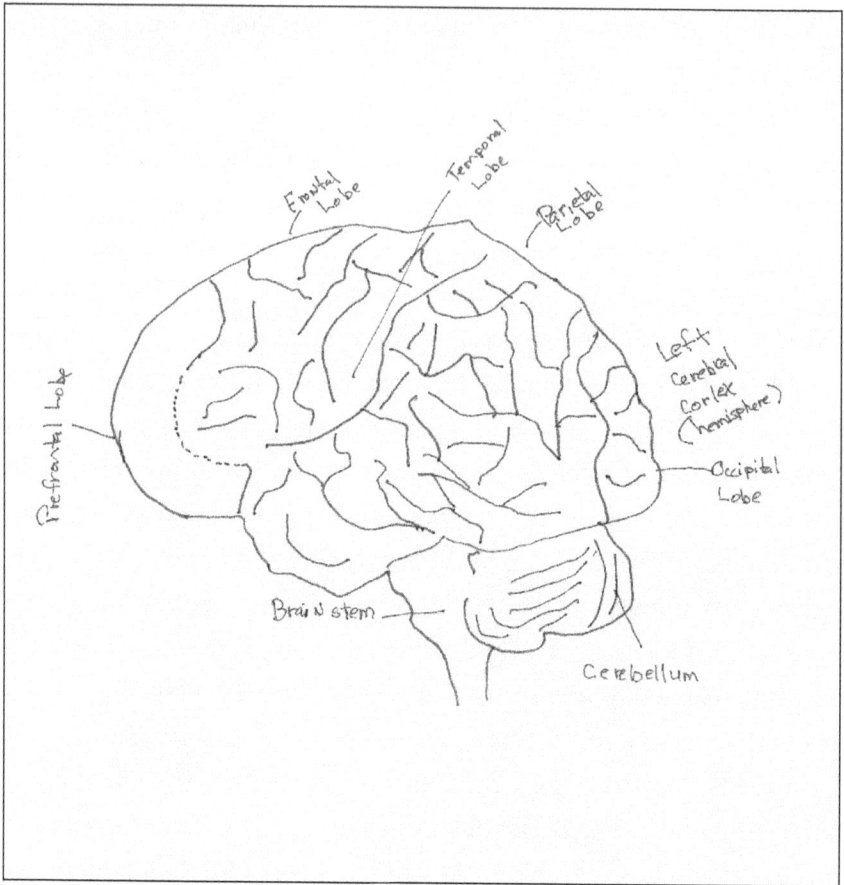

Figure A2.3 External view of human brain, left side, showing the divisions of the greatly expanded cerebral cortex, brain stem (medulla oblongata), and cerebellum.

Now, let's take a look inside:

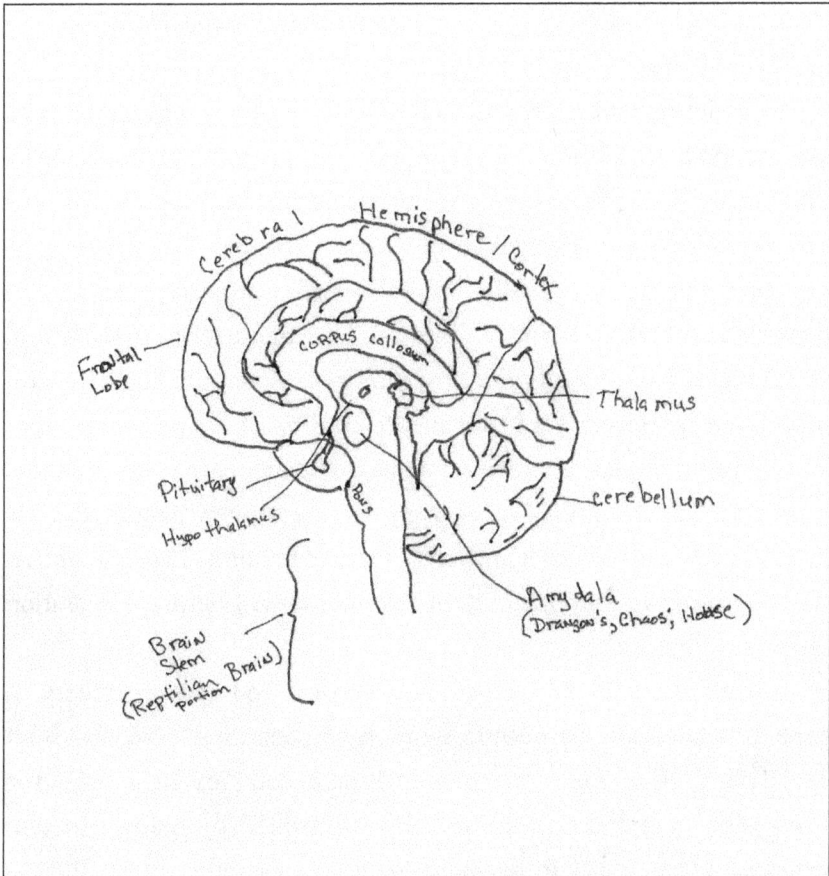

Figure A2.4 Mid-sagittal (through the middle from front to back) view of the inside of the human brain. Now we are looking at the right side, having removed the left side. We will talk about these structures more below in terms of archetypes.

The further down one goes from top (neomammalian), to paleomammalian, to reptilian brains, the brain systems become more "closed," that is, more resistant to environmental variation. They are increasingly programmed to act in specific ways in response to environmental stimuli and changes. Little flexibility is built into them. They remain operating at an unconscious level. Again, it has been estimated that only about 5% of our responses and behavior take place at the conscious level. The other 95% are controlled by unconscious processes. It is in these unconscious levels where the archetypes "live."

Now, let us look closer at archetype evolution. Jung's archetypes are metaphoric, autonomous symbols, with emotional undertones. They evolved in response to real life problems and specific survival and reproductive challenges in our early ancestors. The archetypes' beginnings probably go way back in the vertebrate lineage. They have to do with how we understand, relate to, and orient ourselves in the world.

Drawing from evolutionary psychology and neurobiology, we have reached in recent years a better understanding of Jungian archetypes and the role they play. They were not just a figment of Jung's imagination. Turns out, he was pretty much right on the money. Archetypes are literally built into our genes and have persisted because they are adaptive. As everything else in our human (*Homo sapiens*) heritage, evolution builds on what it already has.

Do our genes code directly for archetypes? Do I have an archetypal gene or genes for Turquoise Woman, for example? No, not that specifically. But like many of our innate complex behaviors, the expression of archetypes is probably controlled by many different genes, acting together in response to environmental cues. Such traits are instinctual, and since we all have these same instincts, they are in our species character, and thus have to have a genetic base. How these genes are individually expressed, however, is different from individual to individual, and depend on the individual's specific genes and environments to which they are exposed. There is a long list of archetypes. Do we even have enough DNA to code for all of these along with everything else it has to code for?

Although we have enough DNA for maybe a million genes, the Human Genome Project, which has sequenced the DNA of the entire human genome, estimated we have some 30,000 or so genes.[59] Additionally, the genomes of many other organisms have been sequenced, from bacteria, to yeast, to fruit flies, reptiles, and mammals.

For all the higher eukaryotes (those above fungi/yeast), this number of genes is comparable. It is not how many genes you have but what and how those genes are expressed. Humans and fruit flies have many of the same genes, differentiated by changes in a few amino acids (the building blocks of proteins). How this limited number of genes codes for all our complex systems, including our many behavioral traits, is still not completely understood. We are making headway. We now know that a lot of what happens in this regard occurs not at the primary level of the gene, but at a secondary and above levels on how the genes are regulated, at the *epigenetic* level. (Epi for above.) Which is probably the level that encompasses the archetypes.

EPIGENETICS, IMPRINTING, AND PREPARED LEARNING

To continue our journey, we may need some basic genetics, a little mini-micro-course. If you already know all this stuff, skip over it.

In general, genes code for proteins. But what does that mean? The DNA double helix molecule is made up of two sugar-phosphate backbones running in opposite directions, hence the name, "double." "Helix" is because of the spiral structure of the DNA, like two intertwined snakes seen in some ancient symbols. Deoxyribose is the sugar. Not something you buy at your local grocery store. I am assuming my readers know what phosphate is. Attached to each sugar is one of four nitrogenous bases: A, T, G, or C, for our purposes here. These bases are the genetic code. This code is read in triplets, called *codons*, that is, it takes three bases to code for a specific amino acid. Amino acids are the building blocks of proteins and proteins are the basic molecules of the body, from muscle to bone to neurons, etc. Additionally, proteins carry on all the biochemical reactions in our bodies. As examples, AAA codes for the amino acid leucine, CCC codes for proline, GCA codes for alanine, etc. There are some 20 different amino acids that our body uses. This is all Nobel-price, Watson-Crick stuff.

To make a protein, the DNA double helix is first unzipped, i.e., the double strands are separated; only one of the strands is read, however. An RNA "message" is made of the DNA. This means the DNA codons are translated into a single stranded RNA message molecule. RNA is basically like the DNA but with the sugar ribose instead of deoxyribose in its backbone. Then this RNA message is used to direct the construction of the protein that it codes for. Simple, no? There are a lot more steps here, but this will again do for our purposes. Okay, now the story gets a little more complicated, because this process is highly regulated.

The expression of the genes is highly regulated in terms of how much of the protein is made and when. So, you have your genes/DNA, and then you have the regulation of those genes. This regulatory level above the gene is referred to as *epigenetic*. Yes, we are still getting to archetypes.

How many copies of a gene's DNA are made into RNA and how many copies of the protein are made from that RNA are highly regulated in our cells. This is the epigenetic level. Let us use a water faucet as a metaphor: the gene (DNA) is the faucet and the water coming out of it, the protein. How much protein/water comes out depends on how open you turn the faucet handle. All the way closed and no protein; all the way open, a lot of protein; anywhere in between, varying amounts of your protein. Each gene is like this, but genes aren't out there all by their lonesome. There is a whole genome full of genes, some 30,000 or so.

All these genes are regulated like an orchestra playing music, with some instruments (genes) playing this, some playing that, some coming in or fading out at different times; loud sometimes, soft at others, etc. Timing is also crucial: all the instruments have to enter and exit at the right time. In our bodies, for example, development of an embryo involves turning on various ensembles of genes in the correct sequence at the right times. These are epigenetic processes. Now we need to talk about learning and the brain.

Learning of any kind is an epigenetic process. Learning depends on the expression of specific genes at the right times. These genes and the proteins they code for then allow neurological growth (neurogenesis), mostly in terms of the connections (synapses or synapsis for singular) between neurons (brain cells). New synapses are laid down, and some are increased. Highly used nerve fibers are increased in diameter so that they become larger and can carry more information, and faster. Similar to muscle building in which muscles you use over and over get bigger and stronger.

Archetypes are epigenetic phenomena. They are an example of what psychologists call *prepared learning* —an inborn predisposition to learn something quickly and decisively—which is a type of *neurological imprinting*. Imprinting is a rapid learning process in which the brains of newborns or very young animals construct a behavioral pattern or recognition, attraction, or avoidance. One example is an infant's attraction to their mother or parents, and avoidance of predators. These become hardwired into their brain, meaning neurological tracks are laid down that pretty much can't be modified afterwards.

Conrad Lorenz's study of imprinting in young ducklings is one of the most famous and earliest imprinting studies. (1937. The companion of the birds. *Auk* 54: 245-273) Young ducklings attach (a.k.a., imprint as their mother) on the first moving thing they see when they hatch. Lorentz was the first moving thing they saw. He became their "mother duck," in that they were rigidly attached to him and would follow him wherever he went. This is a very rigid or inflexible type of attachment, in that once set in place, it can't be undone. It becomes hardwired in their little bird brains. This rigid type of imprinting is seen in most animals. In humans, imprinting is more flexible. Technically, because of this flexibility, it is not imprinting per se, but referred to as *prepared learning*. Something that the brain is set up to learn rapidly similar to imprinting, but more flexible.

Another little tidbit about archetypes, neurologically: we know that when certain areas of the brain are electrically stimulated, subjects reported seeing archetypal-like images.[60] In the brain, the research suggested, archetypes "live at" the junctions of the temporal and occipital lobes, mainly in the right brain (side) of our cerebral cortex. If this "right brain" address is valid, it explains why we can access our archetypes in altered states of consciousness when the right brain is more active, and the more linear left cerebral cortex is less active.

WHAT IS CONSCIOUSNESS?

Let us move on and discuss consciousness and mind for a deeper understanding of how we, *Homo sapiens*, have come to use archetypes. Our consciousness rests upon a structural hierarchy of our underlying unconscious processes. These unconscious processes do not depend upon on the conscious processes. Consciousness, however, could not exist without these underlying unconscious processes. And consciousness is fragile. It can easily fall apart with trauma, disease, drugs, and other stressors. When that happens, we revert back to our instinctual behaviors, and thus enter the archetypes. (When all else fails, call an archetype!)

Consciousness, residing as it does in the cerebral cortex and higher brain centers, is very much open and flexible to environmental learning. It is said to be *domain-general*. In contrast, the older, unconscious systems in the lower parts of the brain, the "old" reptilian and paleomammalian brain wherein live the archetypes, are more universal and closed in terms of environmental learning; they are said to be *domain-specific*. By "domain-specific," I mean we learn some things more easily than other things; e.g., we learn predator detection and social exchanges more easily than, say, calculus. These learning programs are problem specific. Our brains appear packed with a number of domain-specific programs that are cued by specific environmental stimuli/problems. These unconscious systems are able to dominate conscious processing and are "called up" in times of stress or danger. Consciousness, a function of the cerebral cortex and especially the pre-frontal lobe, has a more difficult time dominating them. When we act instinctually, we are acting from an archetype.

Consciousness is domain-general, but it is *unitary*: it only handles one thing at a time. (This is why multitasking is not really an accurate term; we are actually switching rapidly from one thing at a time to another when we "multitask.") Underlying consciousness is a myriad of unconscious domain-specific neural systems, each with their own learning programs and level of "consciousness." All these unconscious systems must compete with each other to gain access to our unitary consciousness for us to become aware that there is an issue or problem that needs to be dealt with. Enters emotions.

MIND

What we call mind is set of domain-specific programs that organize our experiences, along with our genes and universal aspects of the environment. Mind is full of content-rich, domain-specific programs that are specialized for solving specific ancestral problems.

EMOTIONS

Emotions are important evolutionarily, archetypically, neurologically, and spiritually. Emotions are here because they were adaptive: they were key to our species' survival to meet specific challenges for survival and reproduction. They are our motivators that had, and have, critical survival and reproductive value. Basically, emotions motivate us to embark on any learning journey, including a spiritual journey.

Emotions are why we do things. They make us want to get up and take action—or not, to just sit there paralyzed. Emotions are how we make choices, how we choose between one thing or another. When we don't have any feelings one way or another, it is hard to make a decision. (How did Spock on *Star Trek* ever decide what he wanted for lunch?)

OK, emotions evolved because they gave us higher survival value. But, we might ask, that was way back when—what about now? I would argue that emotions are important in today's techno-cultural, overpopulated, over polluted, setting on the pandemic-stressed, deteriorating environmental globe, where our very survival as a species, and myriad other species, stands on the edge of extinction. Not to be paranoid, but things don't look good, folks—if you are paying any kind of attention at all. Hell, just surviving on the Interstate these days is a challenge. Then we have all the crazies running around shooting people and using plastic straws, burning the Amazon rain forest—on and on goes the list.

We have enough smarts to get ourselves into trouble, but not enough to look ahead and take the necessary actions to get us out of the trouble. But, while emotions may not serve us as they did our ancestors in some ways, we dare not try to get rid of them. I would also point out: we can learn how to consciously make use of our individual archetypes and better use of our emotions to help us navigate our complex lives even today. Survival is still important. We are a species waiting for Mother Nature's other shoe, natural selection, to drop.

Both emotions and the archetypes operate primarily at the subconscious level—unless we work to become conscious of them. Emotions enable us to rapidly assess an environmental situation. They get our conscious brain's attention, that is, rise to the level of our consciousness, when raised to a high enough level. If the threat level is high enough, they will bypass consciousness all together and kick in our defenses.

Our emotions go back evolutionarily to basic approach-avoidance mechanisms found in most living organisms: from taxis (movement) in single cell mobile organisms, to tropism (growth) in non-mobile organisms, from bacteria to plants. Because there are a lot more things that can harm you than help you, there are more negative emotions than positive emotions. Emotions of fear and anger are very primal. They can almost instantaneously tell us (consciousness) to pay attention! A saber-toothed tiger is charging us! Run! No thought required. That is, no conscious thought required. Emotions are underpinned by specific but universal psychobiological mechanisms, that is, specific neural circuitries. Our primary archetypes, the more important ones, are tied to these emotional neural circuitries. While the archetypes are not these circuits, our most important archetypes are closely linked to them.

EMOTIONS VERSUS FEELINGS

Emotions are the underlying psycho-physiological responses of our body-mind. They operate automatically and are at the subconscious level. Feelings are our conscious awareness of those emotions. We are often only vaguely aware of our emotions until they get intense enough and break through into our consciousness. It is a common stereotype, still hotly debated, that males in our culture are usually less aware of their emotions than females. With a little practice, however, even us males can become better aware. I often help my clients become more aware of their emotions by asking them where they feel those emotions in their bodies, what does it feel like, is it constant or does it fluctuate, etc.?

EMOTIONAL NEURAL CIRCUITS

Our emotions are based in ancient, highly conserved, older brain regions. I want to emphasize again that these circuits come up rapidly and unconsciously, especially the fundamental ones. There appear to be four fundamental motivational circuits: SEEKING, FEAR, RAGE, and PANIC. FEAR and RAGE are linked to our amygdala and are the center

165

for our flight-or-fight response, and of course, our felt emotions of fear and anger. There are also three more specialized circuits: PLAY, CARE, and LUST. Let's take a deeper dive into each of these.

Again, these emotional neurocircuits are associated with the archetypes, but they are not the archetypes per se.

Each archetype involves a complex of these circuits. Our Shadow archetype, for example, is brought up by our RAGE and FEAR circuits. Shadow is about anger and aggression when we feel threatened or unsafe, when our resources, mates, children, people we care about, etc. are threatened or in danger. Shadow is associated with our primitive drives for survival and reproduction. That is why Bandido is one mean hombre, or can be.

How do my other archetypes fit into this neural circuitry schema? Keep in mind, these are my speculations. Turquoise woman I would guess involves SEEKING, LUST, and CARE circuits. She is a mix of mate and mother symbolism. Warrior is a symbol of self: a self that is strong, capable, and courageous. As such, a counter to the anger and aggression of Bandido. If Warrior exerts aggression, it is a controlled anger. Pushed too far though, and RAGE kicks in. He is prefrontal lobe overcoming or mitigating the primitive emotional responses. VISIONARY is about SEEKING. Finally, Teacher/Guru/Charles in my story is about wisdom, again SEEKING, CARE, and prefrontal lobe and higher brain override. He is more like the Jungian Father archetype.

With the above as a preamble, below is a greater description of the individual neural circuits:

SEEKING

The SEEKING circuitry, a fundamental system found in all mammals, is a dopamine-driven self-stimulatory system of the hypothalamus. In humans, this system engages the higher brain systems and is a major player in forethought as a result. Forethought, looking ahead and planning for some future event, is a very human attribute. It is linked to our pattern-finding circuitry in the prefrontal cortex and hippocampus. When activated to extreme, schizophrenia can result— i.e., seeing patterns where none exist. Our brain is a pattern-seeking/ making machine. The SEEKING system motivates organisms to explore, be curious about or interested in. It also activates expectancy, corresponding to "intense interest," "engaged curiosity," and "eager anticipation." It environmentally engages our "aliveness." Activation stimulates theta brain waves associated with information processing and simulates REM sleep. Cocaine and amphetamines stimulate this system. In terms of importance for basic survival and reproduction, next to flight-or-fight avoidance circuitries, is the SEEKING circuitry. It is the most primal on the attraction side of the attraction-avoidance schema. SEEKING-like circuitries are found in fruit flies and roundworms, for example.

Interestingly for our purposes, the SEEKING system is associated mythologically with such metaphors as the wellspring of life and tree of life (remember Adam and Eve of Genesis), and with the lower worlds of shamanic and indigenous peoples, from whence energy, life, power, and animal archetypes emerge. It is the place of creative beginnings and origins.

When we cannot find what we seek, even if we are not sure what we are looking for, that is, when our SEEKING is thwarted, depression and dysphoria can result. SEEKING is also closely linked to the LUST and RAGE systems.

RAGE

Thwarting of the SEEKING system, along with pain and aggravation, can activate the RAGE system's circuitry. This system evokes angry, aggressive attack behaviors, and is again located in the hypothalamic/amygdala areas of the old brain. Feelings of intense rage occur when this area of the brain is electrically stimulated. It colors our perception and judgment and calls up related feelings and memories. Anger comes up and plans for revenge begin to be conceptualized. The RAGE system has homologies in other vertebrates. As I think about my long zoological career with everything from fruit flies to fish to lizards and birds, mice, rats, dogs, cats, and horses, attacks and aggression are the norm, except for the fruit flies, when it comes to competition for food, mates, territories, and pecking orders. So, RAGE homologies pretty well cover vertebrates in general.

FEAR

FEAR, like RAGE, involves the amygdala and hypothalamus, and additionally the lower brain stem and spinal cords, and can result in profound escape and avoidance behaviors. It activates the startle and freeze responses in its extremes—you know, like possums playing possum or deer freezing in headlights.

The amygdala stimulates the hypothalamus to cause stress hormones to be released from the pituitary (cortisols) and adrenal (epinephrine and nor-epinephrine) glands. These kick in the body's autonomic sympathetic system that controls heart rate, breathing, and blood pressure; voiding the colon and urinary bladder; diverting the blood flow from internal organs to the arms and legs in preparation for flight; and suppressing the immune system. The pre-frontal lobe meanwhile evaluates the danger of the situation, feeding back to the hypothalamus. Fear responses to specific stimuli are quickly learned thanks to the amygdala. When another similar stimulus is encountered, these memories and feelings are quickly brought back up. The pre-frontal cortex is critical in unlearning these responses as well and is what we work with in mental health therapy.

PANIC

Again, another important evolutionary holdover from our reptilian heritage evolving from reptilian pain circuits is the PANIC circuitry, which calls up feelings of social isolation and separation distress. Not a big deal for reptiles, who are pretty much loners, but a really big deal for humans with their extensive social network wiring.

PANIC is about repairing or building social links, reflecting the tremendous importance of social systems in *H. sapiens* with our extended infant care. *H. sapiens* have a highly integrated emotional system for attachments. Reflected in the failure-to-thrive syndrome in newborns and Radical Attachment Disorder, failure to form empathetic circuitry, leading often to Conduct Disorder in teens, and Antisocial Personality Disorder in adults. The PANIC system located in the hypothalamus and other areas of the reptilian brain that involve circuitry running from the amygdala and preoptic area, is closely linked to circuitry for sexual and maternal behaviors as well as pain. Extended social isolation produces panic, anxiety, and eventual depression. When satisfied, the organism releases endorphins, our natural internal opioids.

PLAY

The PLAY circuitry is very mammalian, motivating mammals to engage in rough-and-tumble activities. It promotes social bonding. As we know from watching children and young mammals, this activity arises spontaneously early in development. It is an innate, hardwired function of the mammalian nervous system. It is the source of exuberant joy and extends to being tickled, along with play sounds, which includes human laughter. Overactivity of this system is implicated in attention deficit hyperactivity disorder (ADHD) and mania. With PLAY we have moved from the hypothalamus to the thalamus.

LUST AND CARE

These two circuits have to do with the reproductive component of evolution. The others above are mostly concerned with the survival component.

The LUST circuitry is all about mating, i.e., sexual reproduction. While the LUST circuitry is about sex in general, i.e., you just want to have sex with someone, some affective psychologists split it into two sub-circuits, one for general lust as discussed, and a second for lust for a particular, specific someone.

LUST is about sex drive or libido with a craving for sexual gratification and is associated with estrogens and androgens, the sex hormones. In humans, testosterone drives this circuitry in both sexes. Although involving the amygdala and hypothalamus, higher cortical brain centers as well as SEEKING are involved.

CARE is about parental care, primarily, and others, secondarily. Origins in the hypothalamus, parental care examples can be seen from fish (mouth breeders, sea horses) to reptiles (crocodiles), and all birds and mammals. In parental care, the Mother and Father archetypes are embedded. The archetype of the Madonna with child is an example of a CARE archetype.

ARCHETYPES, LEARNING, AND SPIRITUAL JOURNEYS

In sum then, archetypes are symbols that help us understand things, often ineffable, that are difficult to grasp, acting as metaphors for the unconscious emotions, to make them easier to comprehend. They are easier to understand because they are innate, that is part of our species' heritage, primarily, or secondarily, our own personal history, and are hardwired into our brains or quickly learned. They are dynamic, three-dimensional, and are stand-alone mental constructions, with emotional content, not just abstract symbols. They are, consequently, experienced as external. Archetypes are experienced in altered states of consciousness, such as dreaming, meditation, trances, etc., when the brain can access its deeper, more universal layers.

APPENDIX 2
CHAOS THEORY AND SELF-ORGANIZATION

CHAOS THEORY WAS THE PIONEERING WORK OF I. PRIGOGINE, WHO examined thermodynamic systems not in equilibrium.[61] But the systems he studied were only slightly out of thermodynamic equilibrium. The classic laws of thermodynamics are stated for equilibrium systems. These systems are closed, or isolated, meaning no energy or matter passes in or out of them. They are idyllic, theoretical systems. Natural systems are non-equilibrium, or *open systems*, and energy or matter moves in and out of them. What Prigogine did was to study mathematically the behaviors of non-equilibrium systems, specifically those that were not quite in equilibrium, but not too far from it either.

His work was subsequently expanded to the behavior of open systems far from thermodynamic equilibrium by Jarzynski and Crooks,[62] which includes most of the universe, including, for example all living systems, ecosystems, and many more. These systems are strongly driven by external energy sources, e.g., sunlight. At the time of Jarzynski and Crooks' work, the behavior of such strongly driven systems far from thermodynamic equilibrium could not be predicted. These authors showed that the entropy produced by a cooling cup of coffee, as an example, was simply the ratio of the probability that the atoms in the cup will undergo the process of cooling divided by their probability of going the reverse process. The latter means the atoms will spontaneously interact to heat up the coffee; a very, very low probability. As entropy production increases, so does the ratio, and a system's behavior becomes more and more irreversible.

On the surface, natural living systems seem to violate the laws of thermodynamics, mainly the second law about entropy. Entropy is a measure of the energy available in a system to do work. The greater the entropy, the less the energy available for work. Its inverse is a measure of chaos, or randomness, in the system, which is energy that can't do work. The second law states that in a system, entropy will increase as work is done.

Natural systems, like our body, require continual input of energy. Such natural systems are far from thermodynamic equilibrium, require continued input of energy, and give off heat to their surroundings. They are also *non-linear* systems. By non-linear, I mean that they do not respond in a linear manner to changes in the system. Most of nature is non-linear.

In a linear system, output is proportional to input. In a non-linear system the output is not proportional to the input. Linear systems are easier to understand and predict. In a linear equation, for example, the variable x is actually x to the power of 1 (x^1), whereas x to anything higher, x^2, x^3, $x^{\cdots}$, is non-linear. Likewise, x=y, or x=2y, etc., in a linear system, as long as x is not raised to any power other than 1. However, $x=y^2$, is non-linear.

Let's take throwing a rock while riding on my horse, Apache. It is a linear equation to figure out that the velocity of the rock is just the sum of how hard I throw the rock and how fast Apache is running. i.e., x+y= rock's velocity. It is simple addition. However, what if I am throwing a paper airplane. Whoa! That's a horse of a different color. The complex aerodynamics of the plane, its shape, the wind, etc., make this a much more complicated equation to solve. You would need to use calculus, differential equations, and so forth, because this now is a very non-linear equation/solution.

Our left brain attempts to linearize our very non-linear universe. It is specialized in linear, logical solutions to non-linear problems. Our right brain, in contrast, is better at dealing directly with nature's non-linearity. Take throwing that rock for example and trying to hit a target. My left brain tries to give me a linear solution. But if it is windy or turbulent, or the rock is irregularly shaped, etc., it is difficult to come up with a really linear solution. So, the right brain kicks in and tries to take into consideration the gusts to make my aim better—this ability is very important if you are hunting lunch or trying to drive off a predator. But wait, there is another little caveat here: many systems are approximately linear over a certain range, but beyond that range, becomes non-linear. In a non-linear system, a small change in one variable can result in a large change in another variable.

Take population growth and doubling time. Over a certain population growth range, the doubling time, that is, the time it takes for the population to double, is approximately linear. However, after the population passes a certain size, its doubling times starts increasing exponentially. This was how the mathematician Malthus' formula on population growth helped lead Darwin to his theory of evolution by natural selection. Darwin reasoned that if Malthus was right, shouldn't the world be overrun with living beings? He then went on to reason that some force must be culling many of these offspring. And, what or who would be culled? Those that survived and reproduced less well. Enters natural selection.

Ok, let's come back to Prigogine's work and chaos theory. Order in the universe is not accidental. Darwinian natural selection, along with self-organization, creates, defines, and orders our universe. Simple chemical systems spontaneously self-order themselves: no divine intervention needed. Oil droplets in water and snowflakes are examples.

At a deeper level, cell components will self-assemble, DNA being one of them. Even simple virus components in solution and under the right conditions, spontaneously assemble into a viable virus particle. Order is inherent in the very nature of matter and energy.

Living systems teeter on the edge of chaos and order. Too much chaos and they go over the edge, too disorganized to function. Likewise, too much order and they cannot adapt and respond to changes in their environment. Laws of complexity spontaneously generate much of the complexity in the universe.[63]

Laws of Complexity/Self-organization

Self-organization is inherent to nature; it is part of the nature of the universe. Take our dust devil example earlier. A dust devil simply self-organizes out of the wind and conditions that are present—the physical factors and dynamics at work. When these conditions change, it falls apart or disorganizes or dissipates. There is no Supreme Being out there that made it come into existence. Merely the forces and laws of nature.

The dust devil reminded me of the Biblical Job's whirlwind in which the voice of Yahweh asked Job, where was Job when He, God, created the universe? For those that did not catch the prequel, God had made a bet with Satan that Job wouldn't break, despite His allowing Satan to torture Job, murder his family, and lose everything. How dare Job complain, God was saying! Anything God wanted to do, no matter how terrible, should be just OK with Job.

So it is with natural laws; they are laws that exist by themselves. They come out of the physical and chemical properties of matter and energy. But who made those properties you might ask? This goes back to Plato's First Cause. Theists would argue that God is First Cause, that God created the laws. But then, who created God? Secularists would argue that there is no need for First Cause. The universe has always been as it is. I tend to agree with the latter view as it makes more sense scientifically. No evidence yet exists to support the former view.

Another example of a non-linear system and self-organization is a boiling pot of water. If you take a pot of water and put it on a flame to boil, little bubbles will begin to form on the bottom of the pot as it comes to a boil. If you keep watching, you will notice as more and more bubbles form, the bubbles are not randomly distributed over the pot bottom, but instead take on a type of order or structure. That is, they will self-organize. They may look like a small city as you look down on them, some with tall "buildings" made from columns of bubbles. Some of them will be grouped together. Then there will be places that no bubbles are produced. We say the system, the boiling pot of water, in this case, has self-organized.

Whenever a system is approaching a point of instability, however, that is, conditions are changing so that the system is becoming less stable, the system is more sensitive to small perturbations. Enters the *butterfly effect*, another important component to chaos theory and understanding our spiritual quests.

THE BUTTERFLY EFFECT

The butterfly effect is often explained, for example, as a butterfly flapping its wings in South America, and affecting the weather in, say, Chicago. The concept, introduced by Lorenz in 1972 (no, not the one that was walking the baby ducks), was that small initial starting conditions can have dramatic effects on a system.[64] Of course, any instance or moment is the start of the next moment and its events. So more generally, the butterfly effect says that small perturbations can cause catastrophic changes and reorganization of a system when the system is at a point of instability. This is because what happens in Chicago and what happens in South America are not linearly related, but they still affect one another. Again, this is for systems sitting on the edge of instability.

In our boiling pot example with its bubbles and organization, if you turn up the heat or destabilize the system in some way, you will notice that the organization starts wobbling a little. It is becoming unstable. At such unstable points, you can tap on the side of the pot or drop something into the water, and the bubbles, or system, will reorganize into a new structure. The tap on the pot's side is referred to as a perturbation, and this is our "butterfly."

For our dust devil, maybe the wind shifted up or down in intensity a little. The dust devil approached a point of instability, having trouble keeping its organization. It is at such points of instability that systems are most sensitive to small perturbations or "butterflies." So, there is a "dance" that goes on between perturbations to a system and self-organization.

This is analogous to our spiritual journey and intense experiences. It is a dance between small perturbations and self-organization in our mental processes. "Aha" moments in which we have sudden insights or understandings can lead to self-reorganization of mind. The "Aha" insight is the butterfly in this case. The application of the butterfly effect and self-organization is well known in psychotherapy, especially hypnotherapy.[65]

From a system's perspective, patients are poised in an unstable point when they come into therapy; they are stressed, suffering, or in discomfort. The great hypnotherapist, Melton Erickson was a master at using shock or surprise to disorient (destabilize) the client psychologically.[66] That was his butterfly. He would then follow with a hypnotic-type suggestion that would lead to self-reorganization and healing. Likewise, in spiritual quests, this butterfly/self-organization process can play a critical role.

Classically, Zen Buddhism is divided into two great schools, Rinzai and Soto. Enlightenment, referred to as *satori*, kensho, or *samadhi* is the goal of Rinzai Zen, but not so much Soto.[67]

Enlightenment means seeing into one's own true nature, which means intuitively understanding who you are. (This is opposed to understanding cognitively, as most Westerners tend to do.) Each of these two schools has its own approach to enlightenment.

Soto Zen's approach is a step-by-step approach fostered by long hours of sitting meditation (*zazen*). It holds that just to sit is enlightenment. As such, profound enlightenment is not the goal of Soto Zen per se because we are already enlightened.

Rinzai Zen uses a shock approach to enlightenment—think, butterfly effect. Enlightenment is its goal and represents a dramatic shift in our view of ourselves, the world, and our relationship to each of these. Its Patriarch, Ma-tsu (709 – 788 C.E.), is often credited with being the originator of Rinzai's shock enlightenment approach. Chief among his techniques were Zen koans. But other, more physical techniques were also used. Just as in psychotherapy, the purpose of the shock was to stop the left brain, cognitive mind in its tracks, i.e., to destabilize and open the door for self-reorganization/enlightenment.

However, the truth is, even simple, everyday things—seeing a flower; hearing a bell or music; reading a sutra or scripture; a poem; washing dishes; working in the garden—can be a "butterfly." Hence, this is more like Soto Zen's gradual approach. For me, a combination of the two, Soto and Rinzai, seems to work best. But is there a reason I am more drawn to the more dramatic, intense approaches as opposed to the gentler, albeit slower, approaches? Yes, I think, personality and genes."

In terms of personality, I am not very patient. In general, I want to get things done, now and sooner is better than later. Even with unpleasant things, I usually want to go ahead and get them out of the way so I can move on to more pleasant things. In terms of genes, I am an experiential thrill seeker.[68] Novel stimuli do it for me. Repetitive, routine, and boring are not my thing—this includes boring people. This is neurologically a dopamine-driven trait.

Dopamine is our pleasure-seeking neurotransmitter. Studies with twins indicate a large genetic component for this thrill-seeking trait. And a gene, designated D4DR, has been identified that affects this trait: individuals with one form (allele) score higher on a thrill-seeking measure than individuals with the alternative form. Thrill seeking is a complex trait, however, affected by many genes and environment alike.

So, we would not expect a 1:1 cause and effect. Most likely though, I am a carrier of the thrill-seeking form of the gene.

A third issue for me here is my ability to move into altered states of consciousness during these intense experiences. These states can give me broad expanses of insight and understanding that I could not reach in ordinary states of consciousness. They are highly intuitive and non-linear, right brained, and represent ancient shamanic abilities that predate our science and technology. They are a type of intuitive knowing. In today's scientific society, we ignore or even disdain these ancient abilities. They are here, however, because they had adaptive value. Such intuitive experiences must always be evaluated in the light of science, however, and recognized from whence they come; not from gods or angels, Satan or demons, but from our own unconscious.

CHAOTIC, NOT RANDOM

Chaotic systems are chaotic, not random. They are *deterministic* in that if you start the system under the same set of conditions, it will come out the with same results. In contrast, in a random system, each time you start the system, even with the same conditions, it can come out differently.

ADDITIONAL CHAOS THEORY COMPONENTS

Other considerations from Chaos Theory that are relevant to its role in spiritual growth are as follows:

ATTRACTORS

In natural systems, there are places in the system's space that are *attractors*. These are regions that attract the system toward it. Our fitness peaks in adaptive landscapes are examples of attractors. Our guru Charles' peak on his spiritual mountaintop, is an attractor in our story. In non-living systems, say a ball rolling down a hill, the places of attraction are the low points where gravity pulls them. These represent the ball at equilibrium. In nature there are a lot of attractors. In non-living systems, attractors are points of lowest energy and high entropy, that is, thermodynamic equilibrium. In living systems, because of the large flow of energy through the systems, attractors are points of homeostasis or equilibrium. Consider human body temperature. The homeostatic point is around 98.6° F. If you change the body temperature, say in the case of a fever, the body will work to move the body back to 98.6°. Likewise, if you get chilled, the body will start shivering to create heat, to get your body back to 98.6°.

In spiritual systems, too, we have attractors. The teachings of Buddha, Jesus, the Torah, Islam, for example, can all be viewed as attractors whose teachings attract believers to their belief system.

COMPLEXITY

Complexity begets complexity. Spontaneous self-organization and the butterfly effect explain much of the complexity of our world. A slight change in starting conditions can result in radically different results—and complexity grows in terms of diversity and variation. Natural selection can then cull out or select for those best adapted to their conditions.[69] As complexity builds, more complexity can then be built upon it. Think of the first computers and now all the technology and inventions that have spun off from those early computers. Or the evolution of life, where from an organic chemical soup, we got RNA and DNA, then cells, then tissues, organisms, etc. Or look at Luther's translation of the Bible and the associated printing press technology. From a single church, hundreds of different religious institutions and interpretations, or more, have evolved.

EMERGENCE

As complexity builds and higher levels of organization are generated, laws and interactions governing these higher levels of order emerge. The whole becomes more than the sum of its parts. We start at the level of the laws that govern subatomic particles and energy in physics. As complexity builds at this level, we come to the chemical level and the laws that govern chemical reactions. As complexity of chemical systems builds, we come to sufficient complexity of the cell. Cells form tissues, tissues form organs, on up to individuals. Individuals form populations. Species, ecosystems, planets, and the list goes on. All the laws from the lower levels still apply at the higher levels, but these higher levels have their own laws that apply to them as well.

DIVERSITY AND VARIABILITY

Chaos theory explains, on one hand, the recurrent patterns that are seen in nature, and, on the other, the incredible variability seen in nature.[70] A complex mathematic theory, it enables us to predict patterns and behaviors in complex systems, but not details. Chaos theory describes life as we really experience it. Variability and diversity run rampant in nature. One of the major findings of evolutionary biology the last fifty years has been about the extensiveness of naturally occurring genetic variation in populations from viruses to *Homo sapiens.*

END NOTES

1   Sams, J. and D. Carson. 1999. *Medicine Cards*. St. Martin's Press, NY.

2   Gehlbach, F.R. 1993. *Mountain Islands and Desert: A Natural History of the US-Mexico Borderlands*. pp 10-11. Texas A&M University Press, College Station, TX.

3   Mitchell, S. 1988. *Tao* XE "Tao" *Te Ching*. HarperCollins.

4   Yardley, D.G. 2000. *WindWalker: Journey into Science, Self, and Spirit*. LifeQuest Press.

5   Toole, E. 1999. *The Power of Now: A Guide to Spiritual Enlightenment*. New World Library.

6   Roshi, W. E. N. (2017). "Hold to the Center! Zen XE "Zen" advice for when things blow up around you. *Tricycle*: The Buddhist Review.

7   Firewalking is the act of walking over hot coals or rocks barefooted and dates back to the Iron Age in India to about 1200 BCE. https://en.wikipedia.org › wiki › Firewalking.

8   Jung. C. 1971. *The Portable Jung*. J. Campbell editor. Penguin Books.

9   Castaneda, C. 1991. *Tales of Power*. Washington Square Press.

10   I am using my own version of A. Arriens' medicine wheel. Each direction (north, east, south, and west) has its own archetype and credo. (1993. *The Four-Fold Way: Walking the Path of the Warrior, Teacher, Healer, and Visionary*. HarperSanFrancisco.)

11   MacLean, Paul D. 1990. *The triune brain in evolution: role in paleocerebral functions*. Plenum

12   Fox, M. 1983. *Original Blessing*. Bear.

13   Capra, F. 1975. *Tao* XE "Tao" *of Physics*. Shambala.

14   Jung, C. (editor) 1964. *Man and His Symbols*. Dell.

15   Kolondy, R, V.E. Johnson, and W. H. Masters. 1966. *On Sex and Human Loving*. Little Brown and Co.

16 Myss, C. 2001. *Sacred Contracts: Awakening Your Divine Potential*. Harmony Books.

17 see Jung, 1964; Jung. C. 1971. *op. cit.*

18 Locke, R.F. 1992. *The Book of the Navaho*. 5ᵗʰ edition. Mankind.

19 Jung. C. 1971. *op. cit.* pp139-162.

20 Goodwyn, E. 2012. *The Neurobiology of the Gods: How Brain Physiology Shapes the Recurrent Imagery of Myths and Dreams*. Routledge. pp 43-44 and references therein.

21 Zen XE "Zen" koans are mental puzzles used during meditation to help the student reach a deeper level of truth, usually given in baffling language. There is no logical way to reach the answer and its greater truth. For example, "What is the sound of one hand clapping?" or "What was your face before your mother was born?"

22 Goodwyn, E. *op cit.* p79.

23 Tennyson, A.L. 1850. *In Memorium A.H.H.* Darwin, C.R. 1859. *On the Origin of Species by Means of Natural Selection, or the preservation of favoured races in the struggle for life*. John Murray, London. 1ˢᵗ edition.

24 Grof, S. 2010. *Holotropic Breathwork: a new Approach to Self-Exploration and Therapy*. (SUNY series in Transpersonal and Humanistic Psychology).

25 Darwin, C. 1872. *The Expression of the Emotions* XE "emotions" *in Man and Animals*. John Murray publisher, UK.

26 Rizzolatti, G. and L. Craighero. 2004. The mirror-neuron system. In *Annual Review of Neuroscience*. 27 (1): 169–192.

27 Goodwyn, E. 2012. *op. cit.*

28 Wilson, E.O. 2012. *The Social Conquest of Earth*. Liveright Pub and W.W. Norton & Co.

29 Wilson, 2012. *op. cit.*

30 Dawkins, R. 1976. *The Selfish Gene*. Oxford University. Blackmore, S. 1999. *The Meme Machine*. Oxford University Press.

31 Dennett, D.C. 2006. *Breaking the Spell: Religion as a Natural Phenomenon*. Penguin.

32 From, *The Adventures of Rocky and Bullwinkle and Friends*, cartoons, aired 1959-1964. Dudley Do-Right XE "Dudley Do-Right" was a "dimwitted but cheerful" Canadian Mountie character. Great Saturday morning TV!

33 Alleles are alternative forms of a gene. For example, take the human ABO blood group gene. This blood group gene has three different alleles: A, B,

and O. For any individual, because we inherit one allele XE "allele" from both parents, we can have two alleles that are the same, say, AA, OO, or BB; or, we can carry two alleles that are different, AO, BO, or AB. While an individual has a maximum two alleles, a population can have many more. In a population of humans, you will find the three different alleles (A, B, O) in various frequencies, as explained in text.

34 Attention Deficit/Hyperactivity Disorder.

35 Anderson, W., Th. Dobzhansky, O. Pavlovsky, J. Powell, and D. Yardley. 1975. Genetics of natural populations. XLII. Three decades of genetic change in Drosophila pseudoobscura XE "Drosophila pseudoobscura" . *Evolution* 29: 24-36.

36 See Dobzhansky, Th. 1970. Genetics of the Evolutionary Process. pp 85-87. Columbia U. and references therein.

37 Darwinian fitness XE "Darwinian fitness" explained: actually, in evolutionary genetics instead of fitness XE "fitness" in terms of individuals, which is the *phenotype* that is observed in individuals, fitness is defined in terms of *genotypes, or the specific genes individuals carry.*

38 Kapleau, P. 1980. The *Three Pillars of Zen* XE "Zen" . Anchor/Doubleday

39 May, G. 2004. *The Dark Night of the Soul*. HarperCollins.

40 Rossi, E. 1993. *The Psychobiology of Mind-Body Healing: New Concepts of Therapeutic Hypnosis*. Norton.

41 Jung. C. 1960. *The Collected Works of C.G. Jung: vol 8. The structure and dynamics of the psyche*. (R.F.C. Hull, Trans.). Princeton, Univ. Press.

42 James, W. 1902. *The Varieties of Religious Experience: A Study in Human Nature*. Being the Gifford Lectures on Natural Religion Delivered at Edinburgh in 1901–1902 (paperback), Classics, Library of America.

43 May, G. 1982. *Will and Spirit*. pp 52-68. HarperCollins.

44 Sanchez-Ramon, S. and F. Faure. 2017. The Thymus Neocortex Hypothesis of the Brain: A Cell Basis for Recognition and Instruction of Self. *Front Cell Neurosci*. 2017; 11: 340. Published online 2017:27.

45 Equanimity is also a measure of variance as in statistics. It is a measure of how much our inner-peace varies around its mean (a.k.a., average).

46 Jung, C.G. (1959). *The Archetypes* XE "archetypes" *and the Collective Unconscious* XE "Collective Unconscious" . Princeton U.

47 Capra, F. *Tao* XE "Tao" *of Physics*. Josephson, B. 1987. Physics and spirituality: the next grand unification? *Phys Educ*. 22: pp 15-19.

48 England, J. 2013 Statistical physics of self-replication. *J Chem Phys*. 139: 121923. Wolchover, N. 2014. A new physics theory of life. https://www.quantamagazine.org/a-new-thermodynamics-theory-of-the-origin-of-life-20140122/.

49 Bodanis, D. 2005. *E = mc2: A Biography of the World's Most Famous Equation*. Walker Books.

50 Koithan, M., and D. Farrell. 2010. Indigenous Native American XE "Native American" Healing Traditions. *J Nurse Pract*. 6(6): 477–478.

51 Storm, H. 1985. *Seven Arrows*, p 6. Ballantine.

52 Harris, S. 2014. *Waking Up: A Guide to Spirituality* XE "spirituality" *Without Religion*. Simon and Schuster.

53 Stone, J. 2009. *Religious Naturalism Today: The Rebirth of a Forgotten Alternative*. SUNY, NY.

54 Mesle, CR. 1993. *Process Theology: A Basic Introduction*. pp 127-133. Chalice Press, St. Louis

55 For example, see, Moody, 1975. *Life After Life*. And Brinkley, 2008. *Saved by the Light*.

56 d'Aquili, E. and A.B. Newberg. 1999.*The Mystical Mind: Probing the Biology of Religious Experience*. Fortress Press. p 127.

57 Chida, Yoichi MD, PhD; Steptoe, Andrew. Positive Psychological Well-Being and Mortality: A Quantitative Review of Prospective Observational Studies. *Psychosomatic Medicine*: 70 (7): 741-756.

58 Darwin, C. 1872. *The Expression of the Emotions* XE "emotions" *in Man and Animals*. John Murray.

59 See Human Genome News 1989-2002. https://web.ornl.gov/sci/techresources/Human Genome/publicat/hgn/).

60 d'Aquili, E. and A.B. Newberg. 1999.*The Mystical Mind: Probing the Biology of Religious Experience*. Fortress Press.

61 Prigogine, I. 1997. *The End of Certainty. Time, Chaos, and the New Laws of Nature*. The Free Press.

62 Crooks, G. 2008. Entropy XE "entropy" production fluctuation theorem and the nonequilibrium work relation for free energy differences. *Phys. Rev. E* 60, 2721.

63 Kauffman, S. 1995. *At Home in the Universe: The Search for the Laws of Self-Organization and Complexity* XE "complexity:chaos theory" . Oxford U. Press.

64 Lorenz, E. 1972. *Predictability: Does the Flap of a Butterfly's Wings in Brazil set off a Tornado in Texas?* American Association of Science.

65 Rossi, E. 1996. *The Symptom Path to Enlightenment: The New Dynamics of Self-Organization in Hypnotherapy: An Advanced Manual for Beginners.* Palisade Gateway Publishing.

66 Haley, J. 1993. *Jay Haley on Eric Erickson.* Routledge.

67 Hoover, T. 1980. *The Zen* XE "Zen" *Experience.* Plume.

68 Hamar, D. and P. Copeland. 1998. *Living with Our Genes.* Doubleday.

69 Kauffman, S. 1993. *The Origins or Order: Self-Organization and Selection in Evolution.* Oxford.

70 Kellert, S.H. 1993. *In the Wake of Chaos: Unpredictable Order in Dynamical Systems.* University of Chicago Press.

LITERATURE CITED

Anderson, W., Th. Dobzhansky, O. Pavlovsky, J. Powell, and D. Yardley. 1975. Genetics of natural populations. XLII. Three decades of genetic change in *Drosophila pseudoobscura*. *Evolution* 29: 24-36.

Arriens, A. 1993. *The Four-Fold Way: Walking the Path of the Warrior, Teacher, Healer, and Visionary*. HaperSanFrancisco.

Blackmore, S. 1999. *The Meme Machine*. Oxford University Press.

Bodanis, D. 2005. *E = mc2: A Biography of the World's Most Famous Equation*. Walker Books.

Brinkley, D. 2008. *Saved by the Light*. HarperTorch.

Campbell, J. (ed.) 1971. *The Portable Jung*. Penguin Books.

Capra, F. 1975 *Tao of Physics*. Shambala

Castaneda, C. 1991. *Tales of Power*. Washington Square Press

Chida, Y. and A. Steptoe. 2008. Positive Psychological Well-Being and Mortality: A Quantitative Review of Prospective Observational Studies. *Psychosomatic Medicine: 70* (7): 741-756.

Crooks, G. 2008. Entropy production fluctuation theorem and the nonequilibrium work relation for free energy differences. *Phys. Rev. E 60*: 2721.

d'Aquili, E. and A.B. Newberg.1999. *The Mystical Mind: Probing the Biology of Religious Experience*. Fortress Press.

Darwin, C. 1859. *On the Origin of Species by Means of Natural Selection, or the preservtion of favoured races in the struggle for life*. John Murray, London. 1st edition.

Darwin, C. 1872. *The Expression of the Emotions in Man and Animals*. John Murray, UK.

Dawkins, R. 1976. *The Selfish Gene*. Oxford University. Blackmore, S. 1999.

Dennett, D. 2006. *Breaking the Spell: Religion as a Natural Phenomenon*. Penguin.

Dobzhansky, Th. 1970. *Genetics of the Evolutionary Process*. Columbia U.

England, J. 2013. Statistical physics of self-replication. *J Chem Phys*. *139*: 121923.

Fox, M. 1983. *Original Blessing*. Bear.

Gehlbach, F. 1993. *Mountain Islands and Desert: A Natural History of the US-Mexico Borderlands*. Texas A & M University Press, College Station, TX.

Goodwyn, E. 2012. *The Neurobiology of the Gods: How Brain Physiology Shapes the Recurrent Imagery of Myths and Dreams*. Routledge.

Grof, S. 2010. *Holotropic Breathwork: a new Approach to Self-Exploration and Therapy*. (SUNY series in *Transpersonal and Humanistic Psychology*).

Haley, J. 1993. *Jay Haley on Eric Erickson*. Routledge.

Hamar, D. and Copeland, P. 1998. *Living with Our Genes*. Doubleday

Harris, S. 2012. *Free Will*. Free Press.

Harris, S. 2014. *Waking Up: A Guide to Spirituality Without Religion*. Simon and Schuster.

Hoover, T. 1980. *The Zen Experience*. Plume.

James, W. 1902. *The Varieties of Religious Experience: A Study in Human Nature. Gifford Lectures on Natural Religion* Delivered at Edinburgh in 1901–1902 (paperback), Classics, Library of America.

Josephson, B. 1987. Physics and spirituality: the next grand unification? *Phys Educ*. *22*: pp 15-19.

Jung, C. 1959. *The Archetypes and the Collective Unconscious*. Princeton U.

Jung, C. 1960. *The Collected Works of C.G. Jung: vol 8. The structure and dynamics of the psyche*. (R.F.C. Hull, Trans.). Princeton, U.

Jung, C. (ed.). 1964. *Man and His Symbols*. Dell.

Kapleau, P. 1980. *The Three Pillars of Zen*. Anchor/Doubleday.

Kauffman, S. 1993. *The Origins or Order: Self-Organization and Selection in Evolution*. Oxford

Kauffman, S. 1995. *At Home in the Universe: The Search for the Laws of Self-Organization and Complexity*. Oxford U.

Kellert, S. 1993. *In the Wake of Chaos: Unpredictable Order in Dynamical Systems*. University of Chicago Press.

Koithan, M. and D. Farrell. 2010. Indigenous Native American Healing Traditions. *J Nurse Pract*. 6(6): 477–478.

Kolondy, R, V. Johnson, and W. Masters. 1966. *On Sex and Human Loving*. Little Brown and Co.

Lorenz, E. 1972. Predictability: Does the Flap of a Butterfly's Wings in Brazil set off a Tornado in Texas? *Resonance—J. Science) Education* 20 (3): 260-263.

MacLean, P. 1990. *The triune brain in evolution: role in paleocerebral functions*. Plenum

May, G. 1982. *Will and Spirit*. Harper Collins.

May, G. 2004. *The Dark Night of the Soul*. HarperCollins.

Mesle, C. 1993. *Process Theology: A Basic Introduction*. Chalice Press.

Mitchell, S. (translator and interpreter). 1988. *Tao Te Ching*. HarperCollins.

Moody, R. 1975. *Life After Life*. Bantam.

Myss, C. 2001. *Sacred Contracts: Awakening Your Divine Potential*. Harmony Books

Prigogine, I. 1997. *The End of Certainty. Time, Chaos, and the New Laws of Nature*. The Free Press.

Rizzolatti, G. and Craighero, L. 2004. The mirror-neuron system. In *Annual Review of Neuroscience*. 27 (1): 169–192.

Roshi, W. 2017. Hold to the Center! Zen advice for when things blow up around you." *Tricycle: The Buddhist Review*.

Rossi, E. 1993. *The Psychobiology of Mind-Body Healing: New Concepts of Therapeutic Hypnosis*. Norton.

Rossi, E. 1996. *The Symptom Path to Enlightenment: The New Dynamics of Self-Organization in Hypnotherapy: An Advanced Manual for Beginners*. Palisade Gateway Publishing.

Sams, J. and D. Carson. 1999. *Medicine Cards*. St. Martin's Press, NY.

Sanchez-Ramon, S. and F. Faure. 2017. The Thymus Neocortex Hypothesis of the Brain: A Cell Basis for Recognition and Instruction of Self. *Front Cell Neurosci. 11*: 340.

Schumann W. 1952. Über die strahlungslosen Eigenschwingungen einer leitenden Kugel, die von einer Luftschicht und einer Ionosphärenhülle umgeben ist. Zeitschrift und Naturfirschung *7a*: 149–154.

Stone, J. 2009. *Religious Naturalism Today: The Rebirth of a Forgotten Alternative*. State University of New York Press.

Strom, H. 1985. *Seven Arrows*. Ballantine.

Tennyson, A. 1850. *In Memorium A.H.H.* (Poem)

Toole, E. 1999. *The Power of Now: A Guide to Spiritual Enlightenment*. New World Library.

U.S. Dept of Energy. 2003. *Human Genome News 1989-2003*.

Wilson, E. 2012. *The Social Conquest of Earth*. Liveright Pub and W.W. Norton & Co.

Wolchover, N. 2014. *A new physics theory of life*. https://www.quantamagazine.org/a-new-thermodynamics-theory-of-the-origin-of-life-20140122/.

Yardley, D. 2000. *WindWalker: Journey into Science, Self, and Spirit*. LifeQuest Press.

INDEX

ACKNOWLEDGMENTS

I would like first to thank Strong Eagle, a.k.a.,Lance Crawford, and his sidekick Ernie, a.k.a., Grandfather Chasing Thunder. I never did know Ernie's last name. Next, the Holy Trinity Epsicopal Men's Book Group that read an early version of this book, for the feedback and helpful comments they gave me. Most of these gentlemen were retired university professors (professor emeriti) or professionals: very knowledgeable and helpful. Among them was Fred Sias, PhD, an electrical engineer with a research career and doctorate in physiology. He has been a great help on self-publishing and helped me put together the early version. I would like to thank Patricia T. Pollock for her assistance on that earlier version too.

Finally, I would like to thank my editor and publisher, Rick Benzel, who helped me pull this version together, despite all the science. His ideas on how to organize the chapters and his line editing made a significant difference in developing the final manuscript.. I also thank Julie Simpson, my copyeditor, who really helped to clean up the manuscript, and who just happen to know a lot about Jungian psychology.

ABOUT THE AUTHOR

DARRELL G. YARDLEY, PhD, LPC, IS A LICENSED professional counselor (semi-retired), life coach, Professor Emeritus of Zoology at Clemson University. A retired mental health educator specializing in the neurobiology and genetics of indigenous healing traditions, he is author of *WindWalker: Journey into Science, Self, and Spirit*, and numerous professional papers in evolutionary genetics. His current private counseling practice specializes in equine-assisted psychotherapy for teens. His life coaching practice specializes in parenting troubled teens and in personal and spiritual growth. As an urban hermit, he spends his time writing, gardening, bicycling, cooking, and other activities that promote self-sufficiency, self-reliance, simplicity, mindfulness, and eco-responsibility. For more on Dr. Yardley's writings and work, please visit, www.darrellyardley.com.

www.ingramcontent.com/pod-product-compliance
Lightning Source LLC
Chambersburg PA
CBHW051825090426
42736CB00011B/1648